To: Grampa Hell

11/10/65

From: Marcia Grossi

AMERICA during FOUR WARS

Written by **EARL SCHENCK MIERS** and
FELIX SUTTON

Illustrated by **LEONARD VOSBURGH**
ROBERT DOREMUS
DARRELL SWEET

Design, Layout and Editorial Production by
DONALD D. WOLF and **MARGOT L. WOLF**

GROSSET & DUNLAP • **NEW YORK**

Table of Contents

THE REVOLUTIONARY WAR by Felix Sutton   Illustrated by Leonard Vosburgh

	page		page
The Seeds of Revolution	5	Saratoga	31
The Revolution Begins	9	Monmouth	34
Ticonderoga and Crown Point	12	The American Navy	36
Bunker Hill	13	Vincennes	39
Benedict Arnold at Quebec	16	The Cherry Valley Massacre	40
The Declaration of Independence	18	The British Attack in the South	42
The British Army and the Yankee Army	20	Kings Mountain and Cowpens	45
The Campaign in New York	22	Yorktown	47
Crossing the Delaware	26	Independence at Last	49
Brandywine and Germantown	28	Highlights of the Revolutionary War	50
Valley Forge	29		

THE WAR BETWEEN THE STATES by Earl Schenck Miers   Illustrated by Leonard Vosburgh

Our Country a Hundred Years Ago	52	The Year of Jubilo!	76
The Gathering Storm	55	Lee, the Invincible	78
Six Critical Weeks	58	Grant and Vicksburg	80
War Over a Fort	60	Gettysburg	82
Patriotism	62	Mid-Country	84
Amateurs at War	64	Grant vs. Lee	86
On the Seas	67	The War Takes a Turn	89
Making Naval History	68	With Malice Toward None	92
Professionals at War	70	To Appomattox	94
Fight for the Rivers	72	Brothers Again	97
Maryland, My Maryland	73	Highlights of the Civil War	98

THE FIRST WORLD WAR by Felix Sutton   Illustrated by Robert Doremus

Europe in 1914	100	The Trenches	109
The War in the West to 1917	104	Slaughter at Verdun	111
The German Attack	104	The Bloody Somme	113
The Battle of the Marne	106	1917—"The Fateful Year"	114

	page
The Eastern Front to 1917	115
Offstage in Africa and the Pacific	118
Turkey, Italy, and the Balkans	120
Gallipoli	120
War in the Near East	121
Italy, Rumania, and Bulgaria	123
War in the Sky	125
The War at Sea	129
The Course of the War 1917-1918	134

	page
The Russian Revolution	134
Uncle Sam Declares War	136
The Yanks Go Into Action	139
The Allies Attack	140
The Armistice	142
The League of Nations	143
What Did the War Cost — in Lives and Money?	144
Highlights of World War I	145

THE SECOND WORLD WAR by Felix Sutton   Illustrated by Darrell Sweet

The Years Before the War	148
The Coming Storm	151
The "Quiet" Western Front	155
The Invasion of Scandinavia	158
The Germans Break Through	161
The Battle of Britain	164
The Germans Invade Russia	166
The Arsenal of Democracy	168
Pearl Harbor	169
The Doolittle Raid	170
Battle for the Pacific	172

Guadalcanal	174
The War in Africa	176
The Italian Campaign	178
Advance in the Pacific	180
Invasion of France and Germany	183
The Fall of Berlin	187
Victory in Japan	188
The War-Crimes Trials	189
The United Nations	190
Highlights: 1922-1945	191

THE REVOLUTIONARY WAR

The Seeds of Revolution

The French and Indian War, which ended in 1763, established nearly all of what is now the United States east of the Mississippi River as British territory. The French armies had been driven out of North America, and no longer threatened the northern and western frontiers. Now, the colonists thought, they could devote themselves to the peaceful pursuit of carving a civilization out of the wilderness.

By far, the greater portion of this vast new British land was covered by a carpet of trackless forest inhabited by Indian tribes. Here and there, the British maintained an isolated fort. The thirteen Colonies — New Hampshire, Massachusetts, Rhode Island, Connecticut, New York, New Jersey, Pennsylvania, Delaware, Maryland, Virginia, North Carolina, South Carolina, and Georgia — were strung out in a narrow belt that ran almost the whole length of the Atlantic Seacoast.

These Colonies were prosperous, and were becoming more so with each passing year. Rich farmland was available to any man who had the ambition to clear it. In New England, craftsmen were turning out fine furniture and cabinet work, silverware, soap, candles, leather goods, guns, gunpowder, and sailing ships for the rapidly increasing trade with England. The big merchants were becoming wealthy.

In the South, the owners of great plantations, using slave labor, were harvesting shipload after shipload of tobacco, rice, indigo, and cotton that were sent to the mother country.

Cities sprang up — Boston, New York, and Philadelphia in the North; Williamsburg, Norfolk, and Charleston in the South. Schooners plied on fairly regular schedules between the Colonies. Cleared roads replaced the blazed trails of earlier days. Inns and taverns began to appear along the main highways, assuring travelers of a hot meal and a night's lodging. Guidebooks appeared that indicated the best routes between the larger towns.

Mail routes and stage lines were organized. A stagecoach called the "Flying Machine" made the trip between New York and Philadelphia in two days. The journey between New York and Boston required four or five days.

Every city had one or more newspapers, and these were distributed to outlying villages and towns. Most of the colonists of the upper and middle

Cities sprang up rapidly in the prosperous Colonies. The illustration on the opposite page shows Battery Park in New York City on a Sunday afternoon in the year 1768.

Fine craftsmen were building many sailing ships in New England for the rapidly increasing trade with England. At right, a scene in a Massachusetts harbor.

About 1750: Only a few of the colonists, like Benjamin Franklin (above) and Samuel Adams (at right), thought that America should become an independent nation.

Shiploads of tobacco were harvested by the laborers of the big plantations in the South.

classes could read. Through the newspapers, the people of one colony could learn what was happening in other colonies. A sense of American nationalism began to develop.

Most colonists considered themselves Englishmen and loyal subjects of the King. At this time, only a few colonists, among them the firebrand Sam Adams, had ideas of America becoming an independent nation. Still, the colonists realized that they were different from their English cousins in the old country — in their customs, their way of life, and even in their language. And they called themselves Americans.

These Americans added their own words to the English language, such as *fall* (for autumn), *skunk, hickory, swap, coldsnap, handy, and Yankee.* Outside of the cities, the Americans lived a hard and adventurous life, as opposed to the drab routine existence of the average Englishman back home.

Whether the Americans realized it or not, the seeds of revolution and independence were slowly being planted. The government of the King, across the sea in London, blindly watered these seeds and helped them grow.

The cost of the French and Indian War had tremendously drained the British Treasury. It more than doubled Great Britain's national debt. The yearly budget for maintaining British troops and civil officials in the American Colonies had soared 500 per cent. The British Government felt

The Quartering Act led to the first bloodshed of the Revolution. The incident, which became known in American history as the "Boston Massacre," was triggered off by the resentment of the American citizens against their unwelcome houseguests and hasty reaction on the part of the British.

that, in all fairness, the colonists should bear their share of this financial burden.

Very few leaders in America could argue with this point of view. Unfortunately, King George and his ministers levied and enforced these new taxes in a high-handed way, infuriating the rugged colonists.

The English parliamentary leaders persisted in thinking of the American Colonies merely as possessions that should remain permanently inferior to England. They felt that the Colonies existed only to provide the motherland with abundant supplies of rice, cotton, indigo, and sugar, and to buy British-manufactured goods at sky-high prices. This one-sided opinion ignored the more liberal arguments in favor of the colonists as put forth by two other Englishmen, William Pitt and Edmund Burke, and eventually resulted in the Americans' fight for independence.

Shortly after the end of the French and Indian War, the British Parliament began to pass a series of tax and trade laws that severely damaged the colonial economy. Colonial leaders protested that they should be allowed to pass their own tax laws, or at least be represented in Parliament. To these requests, King George III turned a deaf ear. After the passing of the Quartering Act and the Stamp Act (1765), the first war cry of the coming Revolution was heard: "Taxation without representation is tyranny!"

The Quartering Act, one of the most difficult laws for the colonists to accept, provided that Americans should support a British army of occupation stationed in the Colonies to enforce the tax laws. American citizens were obliged to take Redcoat soldiers into their own homes, and provide them with food and lodging. In Boston and in other cities, resentment against these unwelcome guests led directly to the first bloodshed of the Revolution.

On the evening of March 5, 1770, a crowd of Boston people were shouting insults at a squad of British soldiers. Small boys began to throw snowballs, and one sentry was struck by a club. Captain Preston, a British officer, brought several men to the sentry's assistance. Suddenly, the soldiers turned and fired their muskets into the crowd, killing four men and wounding several others. The country was horrified at what it called the "Boston Massacre."

On December 16, 1773, the next dramatic incident took place that led the outraged colonists one more step toward war. This was known as the Boston Tea Party. The Townshend Acts (1767), unlike the Stamp and Quartering Acts, had levied a tax on imported goods. But after an American boycott, these Acts were repealed in 1770, except for the tax on tea. This enabled the English East India Company to sell tea in the Colonies more cheaply than American wholesalers could. The American merchants had been bypassed and were enraged.

When three English ships loaded with tea docked in Boston Harbor, a group of men disguised as Indians forced their way on board, tore open the hatches, and dumped the cargo of tea into the water. As they were doing this, thousands of people stood on the dock and cheered.

Dressed as Indians, American patriots dumped chests of tea into the Boston harbor.

The Revolution Begins

The British Government tried to punish the colonists for the tea incident by passing the "Intolerable Acts" (1774), which closed the port of Boston. But these acts only served to unite the colonists. They met at the First Continental Congress in Philadelphia in 1774 to discuss their grievances. The movement for full independence was under way, spurred on by Patrick Henry's famous cry: "I know not what course others may take; but as for me, give me liberty or give me death!"

In the months that followed, anti-British feeling in the Colonies became more and more widespread. When the British ignored the pleas of the Congress, militia units were organized in every Massachusetts town. Volunteers called themselves Minute Men, because they said they were ready to take up arms "at a minute's notice" to protect their freedom. These militia companies began to hide secret stores of guns and ammunition in various places in case they would have to fight.

Early in April of 1775, General Thomas Gage, the British commander in Boston, learned from spies that such a store of war material had been hidden in the nearby town of Concord. He planned to march his army on a secret raid to capture the supplies early in the morning of April 19.

But the colonials, who had more spies in Boston than General Gage had throughout the countryside, quickly learned of his scheme. They planned that when the British Army began to march, church bells in all the surrounding towns would ring to summon the Minute Men to the defense of Concord.

Paul Revere, a Boston silversmith who had become famous as a colonial dispatch rider, was chosen to ride and spread the alarm when the British began their march. Fearing that he might be captured before he left the closely guarded city, he made plans to send a signal to other riders across the river in Charlestown. If the British Army were marching by land across Boston Neck, Revere was to hang one lantern in the tower of the Old North Church. If they were going by water over the Charles River, he would hang two lanterns.

At about ten o'clock on the night of April 18, Revere received word that the British were going to leave Boston by the water route. Accordingly, he had a friend hang two lanterns in the church tower, and then he set out by boat for Charlestown. In his famous poem, "The Midnight Ride of Paul Revere," Henry Wadsworth Longfellow confused the matter of the lantern signals, and so he has misled four generations of school children. Longfellow said that the lanterns were a signal *to* Revere. Actually, they were a signal *from* him.

As an added precaution, Paul Revere sent another rider, a young man named William Dawes, to Concord by way of Boston Neck. Although they had narrow scrapes with British patrols, both riders made it as far as the town of Lexington, about ten miles from Concord. Here the two met, halted briefly to rest their horses, and refreshed themselves with a mug of hot buttered rum at Buckman's Tavern. At Buckman's, they

picked up a third rider, young Doctor Sam Prescott, who volunteered to go the rest of the way with them.

Midway between Lexington and Concord, the three were ambushed by a British patrol. Revere and Dawes were captured, but Prescott made it to Concord with the warning.

When the British Army marched into Lexington, they were met on the Village Green by a small force of Minute Men. Ordered to disperse by the British commander, the colonials refused. Someone fired a shot. Nobody knows from which side it came, but general shooting then began. When the smoke of battle cleared away, eight dead Americans lay on the grass. The rest of the colonials had retreated into the surrounding woods and fields. The British marched on toward Concord.

At famed Concord Bridge, they met a determined band of several hundred Minute Men who had been summoned by the clanging church-bells. Ralph Waldo Emerson immortalized the scene in verse:

"By the rude bridge that arched the flood,
Their flag to April's breeze unfurled,
Here once the embattled farmers stood
And fired the shot heard round the world."

Outnumbered and taken by surprise, it was the Britishers' turn to run. As they retreated down the narrow road back to Boston, the army was kept under fire every step of the way by Minute Men who were shooting from behind trees, barns, rail fences, and stone walls. Had the colonial army been made up of frontiersmen with deadly accurate rifles, instead of farmers with clumsy old-fashioned muskets, it is doubtful that a single redcoat would have survived.

The redcoats halted sometimes, and returned the fire in volleys that were mostly wasted on empty air. They finally reached Boston in the evening, with 273 Britishers lost in battle.

Thus, the first battle of the Revolutionary War ended in a rousing victory for the Yankees, and humiliation for the proud army of General Gage.

Ticonderoga and Crown Point

When the news of the Battles of Lexington and Concord was flashed throughout all the Colonies by special messengers, the bonds of loyalty that held Americans to the Crown became stretched to the breaking point. The war was on! Minute Men by the thousands poured into Cambridge, across the river from Boston. Volunteer companies were formed as far south as South Carolina. Boston, garrisoned by some five thousand soldiers, virtually became a city under siege. All supplies from the surrounding countryside were cut off by the Yankee volunteers.

Ethan Allen, a commander of a Vermont militia company called the Green Mountain Boys, led the next offensive move. Two forts on Lake Champlain, in upper New York State, were used chiefly as ammunition depots by the British. Since they were in such a remote location, both were lightly guarded. Allen determined to capture them and carry off the supplies.

He marched his men over the mountains to the lake, seized as many boats as he could and, on the night of May 10, 1775, fell upon Ticonder-

Ethan Allen ferries his Green Mountain Boys over Lake Champlain in a surprise night attack on Fort Ticonderoga.

oga and captured its surprised garrison without a fight. Two days later, the Green Mountain Boys took Crown Point. They then transported the muskets, powder, and ball to the colonial army outside of Boston. During the following winter, when snow lay heavy on the ground, the big guns from the forts were dragged across the rugged mountains in what was one of the greatest engineering feats of the war.

Bunker Hill

In June, 1775, the Second Continental Congress adopted the growing, but poorly organized, New England Army. They appointed George Washington commanding general.

A volunteer army of more than 20,000 Yankees surrounded Boston on every side. Inside the city, a veteran army of six or seven thousand well-trained British troops were virtually prisoners. The British were well-equipped, but their food supplies were running low. As they looked at the hordes of Americans all around them, the men became restless and eager for some sort of showdown. The British officers, Generals Gage, Howe, Clinton, and Burgoyne, felt the same way.

The scene was set for an epic battle that was one of the decisive turning points of the Revolutionary War. After the battle ended, colonists no longer doubted that the American Colonies must break all ties with Great Britain.

In Boston, the besieged British had decided to occupy and fortify the hills on the Charlestown peninsula directly across the harbor from Boston. But the Americans heard of the plan, and on the night of June 16, 1775, landed on the peninsula, bypassed Bunker Hill, and took Breed's Hill, which was nearer Boston. During the night, Colonel William Prescott had led his regiment to the hilltop and had hastily thrown up some make-shift fortifications from which cannon shells might easily be lobbed into Boston itself.

As soon as there was enough light to see, a British warship in the harbor and British artillery on several hills in Boston opened fire. The bombarding, however, did little damage. Colonel Prescott's force was soon joined by officers and men from a number of other Yankee units. Among these officers was General Israel Putnam, a veteran of the French and Indian War. When he heard the news of Lexington and Concord, he came out of retirement and offered men. General Putnam directed the hasty building of more fortifications.

In Boston, the British high command held an immediate council of war. The decision was made to attack as quickly as possible with a frontal assault on the hill. Command of the attacking force was given to General Howe. He at once began to ferry his men across the harbor to Charlestown.

Even after the costly lesson of the retreat from Concord, the British regulars had nothing but contempt for colonial militia. Now, dressed in full uniform and carrying heavy packs that weighed nearly 100 pounds per man, they climbed over stone walls, struggled through plowed fields, and advanced up the slope as well as they could in precise formation. Realizing that his men were low in powder and cannon balls, Colonel Prescott cautioned them to hold their fire until the oncoming ranks were in range. "Wait until you see the whites of their eyes!" he ordered.

The gleaming white crossbelts of the British made perfect targets.

GENERAL ISRAEL PUTNAM

When the order was given to fire, their ranks were mowed down before the Yankee guns like ripe grain before a scythe. Such punishment was more than the advancing soldiers could take. The redcoats retreated out of musket range.

Once again, they formed their lines at the base of the hill. Once again, they advanced against the Yankees. Once again, they ran up against a deadly stone wall of murderous lead. And for the second time, they retreated in bloody confusion, leaving the slopes littered with the bright uniforms of their fallen comrades.

More reinforcements came from Boston, and General Howe ordered a third attempt on the hill. Again, the slaughter continued. Then, suddenly, the Yankee firing stopped. The defenders of the hill had completely run out of ammunition. They quickly retreated from the hill and went back to the mainland, leaving Bunker and Breed's Hill in possession of the remainder of the British Army.

Some 1500 redcoats had been killed or wounded in the brief, but bloody, engagement. The American dead were 140; the wounded, 271.

Once again, the British generals learned to their sorrow that the American "rabble in arms," as Burgoyne called them, could fight as long as they were supplied with powder and ball.

George Washington, Commander in Chief of the Continental Army, hurried at once to Cambridge. He arrived on July 2, but found supplies so scarce, and discipline in the militia ranks so lax, that he spent the next eight months trying to whip his army into fighting shape. All summer, fall, and winter, Washington worked to turn the volunteers into an efficient fighting force. In the spring of 1776, he decided to drive the British once and for all out of Boston.

Amazingly enough, the British General Howe, who had succeeded Gage as supreme commander, had neglected to fortify the Dorchester Hills that overlooked Boston from the south. Washington now proceeded to fortify them, putting the British Army in Boston at the mercy of his guns. There was nothing for the British to do but evacuate the city.

Although no formal agreement was made, both sides understood that Washington's men would not molest the British while they embarked, if the British in turn left Boston without damaging the city. Thus, on March 17, General Howe's army sailed out of the port of Boston for Halifax, taking with them about one thousand colonists who were still loyal to the King.

The battle at Bunker Hill was bloody. Only after their ammunition ran out did the Americans retreat.

Benedict Arnold at Quebec

While these stirring events were going on around Boston, a brash young officer of the Connecticut militia named Benedict Arnold conceived the idea of a bold attack on the fortress city of Quebec, in Canada. An invasion of Canada, via Lake Champlain and Montreal, was already under way, led by General Richard Montgomery. Arnold proposed to General Washington that he lead an army north through the wilderness of Maine, join up with Montgomery, and surround Quebec.

Since the capture of Quebec would cut off the British northern source of supplies that came through the St. Lawrence River, Washington gave his consent. Arnold at once set out to recruit an army in Maine, New Hampshire, and Vermont.

The march of Arnold's men is a classic in military history. In one of the worst New England autumns in years, he started up the Kennebec River with an army of 1,100 men. They carried their supplies in crude flatboats called bateaux. Cold, snow, and freezing rain dogged them every mile of the miserable way. Dozens of Arnold's followers died of exposure. But he relentlessly continued.

Just south of Moosehead Lake in late October, the expedition moved westward, across the Chain of Ponds, to Lake Megantic and the headwaters of the Chaudière River. From here, they floated down to the St. Lawrence River and Quebec.

For a month after arriving at the St. Lawrence, Arnold rested his weary men and waited for Montgomery, who had taken Montreal and was moving to join Arnold's forces. On New Year's Eve, 1775, in a blinding snowstorm, the two armies made a desperate effort to scale the sheer rock walls upon which the city of Quebec was built. Montgomery was killed, and Arnold was wounded in the knee. After a stiff fight, the Americans were forced to withdraw, but they kept a tight blockade on the city for the balance of the winter.

With the coming of British reinforcements in the spring, Arnold was forced to retreat by way of Montreal and Lake Champlain. He was pursued by General Guy Carleton, who intended to defeat him and then capture upper New York State. When Arnold turned on his pursuer at the Battle of Valcour Island and whipped him soundly, Carlton returned to Canada and New York was saved.

The illustration on the opposite page shows General Montgomery's men following the rocky trail around Cape Diamond. They were finally halted by salvos of cannon fire.

Because of his spectacular march on Quebec, his victory at Valcour Island, and the important part he later played in winning the Battle of Saratoga, Benedict Arnold was soon one of the popular heroes of the Revolution. But, being an extremely vain man, he was offended when he was passed over for promotion. Furthermore, he had extravagant tastes, and was constantly in financial trouble. When he found that he could sell military secrets to the British for large sums of money, his patriotism gave way to greed.

In 1780, while in command of West Point, he arranged to surrender it for 20,000 pounds. When this plan was discovered, Arnold fled to the British lines. He was made a brigadier in the British Army; but the British had no more use for a traitor than did the Americans.

Arnold died in disgrace in England in 1801. History will always remember him, not for his deeds of valour, but for his acts of treachery.

The Declaration of Independence

After the bloody battles at Lexington and Concord, the enthusiasm for independence was further stimulated by Thomas Paine's stirring pamphlet *Common Sense*. He wrote, "These are the times that try men's souls. The summer soldier and the sunshine patriot will, in this crisis shrink from the service of their country. . . . Tyranny, like hell, is not easily conquered." Washington had the pamphlet read aloud to his soldiers, and more than 100,000 copies were sold.

The American Congress still made one attempt toward reconciliation by sending a final petition to King George. Called the Olive Branch Petition, it sought once again some way by which England and her American Colonies could find a solution to their mutual problems.

The King's reaction was one of contempt. He at once declared that the Colonies were in a state of armed rebellion; and Parliament followed this with a new act forbidding all trade with the 13 Colonies.

The Americans desperately needed war supplies. But by now, the leaders in Congress realized that no foreign nation would trade with them as long as they considered themselves subjects of Great Britain. It was clear that the only hope of securing foreign aid lay in declaring the American Colonies a free and independent nation.

In early June, Congress appointed a committee to draw up such a

After agreement was reached on the main points of the Declaration of Independence, its actual writing was done by Thomas Jefferson.

declaration. Two of the members were Thomas Jefferson and Benjamin Franklin. The committee agreed on the main points to be covered, and then turned the actual writing of the document over to Jefferson. After a number of changes and revisions had been made in Jefferson's original draft, the Second Continental Congress formally adopted the Declaration on July 4, 1776. By the end of the summer, it had been officially adopted by each of the 13 Colonies that now composed the infant United States of America.

Independence Day, John Adams prophesied, would be "celebrated by succeeding generations as the great anniversary festival. It ought to be solemnized with pomp and parade, with shows, games, sports, guns, bells, bonfires, and illuminations, from one end of the continent to the other, from this time forward, forevermore."

And, as we all know, it has been and always will be.

Historians generally consider the Declaration of Independence to be one of the greatest human documents of all time. In ringing phrases, it sets forth a philosophy of government that had never been voiced, a statement of basic principles that no oppressed people had ever dared to say out loud.

It declares three basic truths:

"That all men are created equal; that they are endowed by their Creator with certain unalienable rights; that among these are Life, Liberty, and the Pursuit of Happiness."

"That governments derive their just powers from the consent of the governed."

"That when any form of government becomes destructive of these ends, it is the right of the people to alter or abolish it and to institute a new government."

These simple truths ignited a flame that was soon to spread like wildfire around the world. They sparked the French Revolution, and the revolt of the South American countries against the Spanish and Portuguese kings. Today, their echoes can still be heard in the struggles for freedom among the new nations of Africa and Asia.

Now, with the Declaration of Independence at last adopted, the die was cast. There could be no turning back, even in the unlikely event that the King and Parliament might decide to change their minds and come to terms. The war had to be won decisively. The British Army had to be driven from American shores. Failure was unthinkable. As old Ben Franklin put it so pointedly when he affixed his signature to the Declaration: "Now, gentlemen, we must hang together. Or, assuredly, we will all hang separately." But it was going to be a long uphill fight, and no one knew it better than George Washington.

The British Army and the Yankee Army

The British Army in America in 1776 and 1777 was a formidable fighting force, as reckoned by standards of that day. This army consisted of the 9,000 men that General Howe had evacuated from Boston. More redcoats were detached from service in Ireland and transferred to North America. Convicted criminals from English jails were offered the choice of army service or imprisonment.

King George, realizing that he needed a larger army, hired 30,000 German soldiers and shipped them to the Colonies. Because most of them came from one German state, Hesse-Cassel, these soldiers were commonly known as Hessians.

The Hessians were good troops, well-drilled and well-disciplined. But who could expect them to fight very hard? They had nothing for which to fight. Many of these Germans deserted to the American side, accepted homesteads, and subsequently became successful farmers and loyal American citizens.

Several thousand Loyalist Americans who were opposed to independence fought for the British King. The most famous of these Loyalist regiments was Tarleton's Legion.

The British leaders also sought to enlist Indian tribes to fight against the colonists. For the most part, the Indians hated the colonists because the frontiersmen had invaded their hunting grounds. The British promised that these hunting grounds would be left alone if King George won the war. The Indians harassed frontier settlements. But as reliable fighting men, they were of little or no use. Whenever endangered, they melted away into the forest and disappeared.

George Washington never knew from one day to the next exactly how many men he had in his army. In the first burst of patriotic outrage after Lexington and Concord, some twenty to thirty thousand men volunteered for military duty. But this number rapidly diminished as these "citizen soldiers" returned to their farms to plant or harvest their crops.

Nearly all of the American soldiers were members of state militia units and had volunteered for only a few weeks at a time. When the periods of their enlistments expired, they simply shouldered their muskets and drifted away.

As an ex-officer of the British Army, Washington dreamed of putting together a regular, well-trained American military force. To encourage volunteers, large bounties were offered, including promises of free farmland at the war's end. But the regular colonial army never exceeded more than five or six thousand men.

On the other hand, the Militia Men were always ready to turn out for a few weeks to meet emergencies. The knowledge that they would always be met by large masses of untrained, but determined, farmers kept the British constantly off balance.

British deserters made a small but steady contribution to Washington's army. These men, most of whom could never hope to own property in the old country, were lured by the prospect of free land in the New World, and of a future life in a free country.

Thus, George Washington proposed to win the independence of the new United States with a makeshift army. It was poorly equipped, poorly clothed, and poorly fed. It was outnumbered and outgunned in almost every engagement it fought. It was led by officers who, for the most part, had little or no military training. It was chiefly by a series of lucky breaks, and British blunders, that the American Army managed to win in the end.

The Campaign in New York

After the British commander General William Howe had evacuated his army from Boston in the spring of 1776 and taken it to Halifax, he immediately had set about building it into the biggest fighting force yet seen in America. By June, with the addition of fresh Hessian troops, he had more than 30,000 men, supported by large units of the Royal Navy.

There was little or no question about where Howe would strike next. Almost certainly his objective would be New York City. There were two major reasons for this. In the first place, New York was situated on an island surrounded by navigable water. Its main harbor was the largest in the New World. It would provide the perfect base for England's mighty fleet, and that fleet could protect it on all sides. New York would also be an ideal headquarters for the British Army.

Under cover of a driving rainstorm, a regiment of ex-fishermen from Salem and Marblehead rowed General Washington's entire army across the East River to temporary safety in Manhattan.

Secondly, New York commanded the mouth of the Hudson River. The Hudson leads north to Lake Champlain and Lake George, which are connected by a system of rivers with the St. Lawrence and Canada. If the British could capture and control this water route, they could cut the American Colonies into two halves, and conquer them one at a time. On paper, the plan looked good.

It was not difficult for George Washington to guess what was in Howe's mind. Therefore, as soon as the British had left Boston in American hands, he moved his army to New York. There he began to fortify the city, as well as the hills in Brooklyn across the East River. When Howe made his move, in late August, Washington was waiting for him on Brooklyn Heights.

The battle that ensued was a severe defeat for the Yankees. Outnumbered by about three to one and led by officers who did not know the terrain, they were at last forced to retreat. Nearly a thousand men, most of them taken as prisoners, were lost.

Now General Howe obligingly made a tactical blunder that saved the rest of Washington's army. Instead of pressing his advantage, he halted his men in front of the last Yankee line of defense, and sat there for two days.

Meanwhile a violent rainstorm had come roaring down out of the north. Under the protective cover of its driving fury, Washington collected a fleet of several hundred small boats. He put this little flotilla under charge of a regiment of ex-fishermen from Salem and Marblehead, Massachusetts. As the rain hammered down, these Massachusetts men rowed the entire army across the East River to the temporary safety of Manhattan.

But safety of Washington's army in New York was only very temporary indeed. The British fleet could, and on several occasions did, sail around Manhattan Island unopposed. This meant that British troops could land anywhere on the island and completely cut off New York City, which was then only a small town on Manhattan's lower tip.

New York was entirely undefensible, and no one knew it better than George Washington. He at once made preparation to retreat northward to the mainland of Westchester County.

The army began the evacuation of Manhattan on September 12, taking with them their ammunition and supplies, their sick and wounded. But there was a shortage of horses and wagons, and progress northward up the island was agonizingly slow.

Then, on September 15, General Howe's troops invaded the island from Brooklyn. British warships in the East River opened up with a tremendous barrage that terrified the raw American troops and sent them fleeing northward in panic. Under cover of the gunfire, the British troops began to come ashore from landing barges. The British soldiers, immaculate in their brilliant red uniforms, pursued the fleeing Americans with parade-ground precision.

When he heard the sound of the cannon fire, General Washington and his staff rode south from their temporary headquarters in Harlem, at the north end of Manhattan. When he saw that the retreat had become a rout, the general attempted to stop it and organize a line of resistance. But it was no use. The fleeing men paid no attention. They threw aside

To slow up the British advance, Mrs. Robert Murray, so goes the story, gave a tea party for General Howe and his staff.

everything that might hinder their running — guns, blankets, knapsacks, powder horns, overcoats — and bolted along the road north.

The story is told that Mrs. Robert Murray, a steadfast patriot despite the fact that her husband was a British sympathizer, gave a hastily organized tea party for General Howe and his staff. She wanted to slow up the British advance and give the Americans more time to escape. Whether or not this gave Washington any extra time is debatable.

On the following day, General Washington managed to rally his men for a brief stand on Harlem Heights. Although the British were momentarily stopped, Washington realized that trying to hold Manhattan was a hopeless task. He left a garrison of some three thousand men at Fort Washington, on the Manhattan side of the Hudson, and retreated into Westchester.

Howe followed and, at the Battle of White Plains, on October 28, won another victory. But, again, the British general failed to follow up his advantage and Washington was able to take his men across the Hudson River into New Jersey.

Three weeks later, Fort Washington was attacked by an overwhelming force of Hessians and every man in the fort was either killed or captured. Now all of New York was in British hands, and the remnants of Washington's army were adrift in the hills of New Jersey and Pennsylvania.

Crossing the Delaware

By Christmas of 1776, George Washington's army was all but beaten. Discouraged by an endless series of defeats and retreats westward from New York, the army had finally made camp on the Pennsylvania bank of the Delaware River, just across from the town of Trenton, New Jersey.

In the era of the Revolutionary War, it was traditional that wars were more or less called off during the winter months. Thus, General Howe had taken the main part of his army back to New York to wait for spring. He had, however, left small garrisons in a number of New Jersey towns. One of these towns was Trenton, which was held by three regiments of Hessians.

The British were able to surprise General Anthony Wayne and his troops, encamped at Paoli near Philadelphia. Using only bayonets, the British killed or wounded many Americans; they, however, lost only a few men. (See page 28.)

Washington decided that this was the time to strike a decisive blow, more for the sake of his army's morale than for any hope of a victory that might change the course of the war. He ordered every boat for miles up and down the river to be assembled for an attack. It was to be an all-or-nothing try. His army had only a slim chance to get back across the river if the attack failed. But Washington was willing to gamble.

Christmas night, 1776, was bitterly cold. The Delaware River was filled with large, floating chunks of ice, and the air was a swirl of sleet. Washington's men were dressed in flimsy summer clothes, and most of them wore no boots. Their feet were wrapped in rags for protection against the biting cold. Their footprints left bloody tracks in the snow.

At daybreak, the Americans landed on the Trenton side of the river and charged into the town. Most of the Hessians had been up all night, drinking wine and celebrating the holiday. Before they had time to come to their senses, they were surrounded. Their commander, Colonel Rall, was killed. The entire garrison of about a thousand men was captured.

GENERAL ANTHONY WAYNE

News of Washington's victory lifted the spirits of all the American colonists, and then another victory followed on its heels.

General Charles Cornwallis, who was later to surrender at Yorktown in the final battle that won the war for Washington's army, marched south from his headquarters in Princeton in an attempt to recapture Trenton. Washington lured him on by keeping the Yankee campfires burning; but meanwhile he took the bulk of his army in a surprise march around the British rear. Almost before he knew what was happening, Cornwallis found himself surrounded by shooting, shouting Americans. He retreated towards Trenton, but the rear guard of his army, which had fallen back toward Princeton, was taken prisoner.

Brandywine and Germantown

Colonel Henry Knox made what proved to be a costly mistake when he ordered his men to level Chew Mansion with cannon fire.

After his surprise victories at Trenton and Princeton, Washington took his army into winter quarters at Morristown, New Jersey. Actually, he went with what remained of his army, for most enlistments were up at the end of 1776. Once more, the general was faced with the heartbreaking task of signing up new men.

Washington feared that Howe might attack while he was in the process of forming a new army. But once again General Howe obliged. He kept his army in New York.

Things remained quiet on the New Jersey front until the end of July. By this time, Washington had managed to put together an army of about eight thousand men. Howe then pulled a surprise move by embarking his entire force of 17,000 on a huge fleet of transports and putting out to sea.

Where was Howe going? Washington sweated out the answer to that question for a month. Then the British Army began to make landings on the northern shore of Chesapeake Bay in Maryland, and marched toward Philadelphia, the capital of the United States. Washington quickly moved his men south to head off the British.

The two armies met at the violent Battle of Brandywine Creek, and once again the Americans were outmaneuvered, if not outfought, and badly beaten. Howe captured Philadelphia, and the Continental Congress fled to the town of York, Pennsylvania.

Now Washington planned another surprise attack on the British, this time at their headquarters in the village of Germantown just outside Philadelphia. The battle began well for the Yankees. They closed in on the British from four sides. Then, an American officer made a fatal mistake.

About a hundred redcoats had taken refuge in the Chew Mansion, a large stone house, and opened fire on the oncoming Americans. Instead of going around the house and keeping it behind them, the Yankee commander, Colonel Henry Knox, ordered his men to level the house with cannon fire.

The sudden cannonading and the clouds of powder smoke only served to confuse the advancing Americans. By the time they were able to reorganize, their ammunition was exhausted, and they were forced to retreat.

General Howe now held one of the most important American cities. He and his troops spent a comfortable winter in Philadelphia. Meanwhile, British supplies could be shipped up the Delaware River.

Once again, Washington moved his army into quarters for the winter, this time in Valley Forge, Pennsylvania.

Valley Forge

The winter of 1777-78, which Washington and his men spent encamped at Valley Forge, was one of the most miserable experiences that any army in history ever had to endure. The weather was unusually bitter and cold, and the snow was unusually deep. The men were ragged. Very few had shoes. As they had done at Trenton the winter before they wrapped their feet in old rags for protection, and again left bloody tracks wherever they walked.

Those among the men who had enough clothes to work outdoors cut down trees to make shacks and lean-tos. There were no horses, and the men pulled their own homemade sleds over the snow.

Worst of all, the soldiers were half-starved, an inexcusable situation because many farmers in that part of Pennsylvania had stores of meat and grain in their smokehouses and corncribs. But they refused to take American paper dollars in exchange for it, and Washington had no gold or silver. Even if the farmers would sell some produce, there was no way to transport it safely.

The Continental Congress, then in session in York, Pennsylvania, could do little to alleviate Washington's dire plight. This Congress had no power to tax people or goods. The only way for them to raise money was to borrow it. Congress went deeper and deeper into debt, and these debts could never be repaid unless the Colonies won the war. So they were reluctant to send money if they could not see a quick victory.

But George Washington was determined to keep his little army together, and he stayed with his men at Valley Forge and shared their hardships. Hundreds of his soldiers left when their enlistment terms expired. Others, half starved and half frozen, simply walked off through the woods and went home. But those who had the courage and determination to stick with their commander, became the hard core of a new American Army that was finally to go on and win the war.

Toward the end of the winter, Washington was joined by an unexpected recruit. This was Baron Friedrich von Steuben, a professional German officer who had served under Frederick the Great.

The American soldiers, even though they had been through many battles, had never had any basic military training. Von Steuben now became their drillmaster. He taught them how to march in military formation, how to handle their guns properly, how to execute commands, and, in general, how to conduct themselves like soldiers.

When they next went into action, at the Battle of Monmouth in the following June, they showed that von Steuben's training had paid off. They stood up to the best the British had to offer, and finally won the day.

As if Washington did not have enough to worry about at Valley Forge, a conspiracy against him was brewing in the Congress. It was headed by General Horatio Gates, who was taking credit for the victory over Burgoyne at Saratoga, and General Thomas Conway, a French officer of Irish descent who was on Gates' staff. This plot was known as the Conway Cabal, cabal being an old-fashioned word for intrigue.

The plotters schemed to oust Washington from his command of all American forces and replace him with Gates. The true reasons behind the cabal have remained obscure. But a few facts are apparent. Some officers, like Gates, were jealous of the fact that Washington was the popular hero

Martha Washington visits her husband at Valley Forge.

General Washington meets Baron von Steuben, who volunteered to teach the American troops drilling and maneuvering principles.

Some of Washington's ragged soldiers inside a primitive log hut at Valley Forge.

of the people. Others felt that while Gates had been successful in the crucial Battle of Saratoga, Washington's record was only a series of failures and near-failures. Some Congressmen feared that Washington wanted to eventually set himself up as the King of the United States.

Washington, of course, knew what was going on. But he kept himself aloof from the controversy and devoted all his time to keeping his army together at Valley Forge. If he ever got discouraged and wanted to quit, he did not show it.

The Conway Cabal petered out in the spring, and George Washington once more went about his business of leading his fight against the British.

Saratoga

While George Washington was having his major troubles and minor triumphs in New Jersey and Pennsylvania, the British war office in far-off London set the wheels of its grand strategy in motion. The object was to divide the Colonies in two, and defeat one-half at a time. The plan had three parts.

General John Burgoyne was to march his army of 7,500 British and Hessian regulars down from Quebec by way of Lake Champlain. Colonel Barry St. Leger, with a well-organized force that included 1,000 Indians, would move eastward from Lake Ontario down the Mohawk River. General Howe would bring his huge army up the Hudson from New York City. When the three armies converged at Albany, the northern half of the Colonies would be firmly caught in the net.

But from the very beginning, things went wrong. For some reason, Howe did not receive his orders and, as we have seen, took his army south to Philadelphia. St. Leger's operation went smoothly until he ran up against stubborn resistance by a small group of American militia at Fort Stanwix, a wilderness outpost on the site of the present city of Rome, New York. Vastly outnumbered, it seemed that the defenders of the fort were doomed. The outlook became even grimmer when a party of 800 volunteers, on their way to relieve the fort, were ambushed and all but wiped out by St. Leger's Indians at Oriskany. Then, Benedict Arnold did by trickery what could not be done by force.

He sent a spy into St. Leger's camp, to tell the Indians that an overpowering American force was on its way to massacre them all. The Indians mutinied, seized St. Leger's supplies of whiskey, got drunk, and deserted into the woods. With most of his force gone, St. Leger had to give up and go back to Canada the way he had come.

Meanwhile, General Burgoyne was having his difficulties, too. Known as "Gentleman Johnny," Burgoyne paid more attention to the fine clothes he wore and the fine food that he and his staff ate than to the business of running his army. He knew nothing about fighting in the wilderness and neither did his officers.

At Bennington, Vermont, Burgoyne lost nearly 1,000 men when a raiding party, sent out to steal horses and cattle, was surprised by Yankee Militia Men. A month later, on September 19, 1777, as the cumbersome British column was painfully making its way through the thick forests, it was attacked by an American force at Freeman's Farm and soundly beaten.

Another two weeks passed while Burgoyne sat and tried to figure out what to do. Then the Americans, sparked once more by the dashing Arnold, hit again at a place called Saratoga. This time, "Gentleman Johnny" was finished. When he surrendered to General Horatio Gates, the Yankee commander, the British fighting forces in America had been dealt a staggering blow from which they never recovered. They lost seven generals, 300 lesser officers, over 5,000 men, 27 cannons, more than 5,000 muskets, as well as vast supplies of powder, ball, food, and other stores. Most historians agree that Saratoga was the turning point of the Revolutionary War.

"Gentleman Johnny" surrenders to General Horatio Gates at Saratoga.

33

Monmouth

In the spring of 1778, General Howe resigned as Commander in Chief of the British forces. His army had spent a comfortable winter in Philadelphia while Washington's men had been freezing in Valley Forge. But Howe had become convinced that trying to subdue the American rebels was a hopeless task that could only end in failure. His place was taken by General Sir Henry Clinton.

Clinton's first order of business was to retreat from Philadelphia and take his army back to New York. When Washington learned of this movement, he decided to attack.

By June, Washington had built his strength up to some twelve thousand men. Thanks to the rigorous training program of von Steuben, they were fit and combat-ready. What Washington did not know was that he had a traitor on his staff.

General Charles Lee was an ex-British officer who had joined the American cause. Because of his military background, which Lee had taken great pains to exaggerate, Washington welcomed him and made him second in command. A year before, during the retreat across New Jersey, Lee had been captured by the British. During his term of imprisonment, Lee had decided that the Americans could not win the war and so he became turncoat again. He gave the British a detailed plan for defeating Washington.

General Washington, with saber drawn, at right, relieves General Lee of his command at the Battle of Monmouth and reprimands Lee severely in the presence of the men.

Now, just before Washington was to attack Clinton, Lee was exchanged for an English general and returned to duty with the American Army. Washington gave him back his old job as second in command. Washington's plan was to have Lee take a forward element of the army and attack Clinton's columns. When the British turned to fight, Washington would then come up with the rest of his army and finish Clinton off once and for all.

Lee made his attack, as planned, near the little town of Monmouth Court House in New Jersey. But when the British resisted, also as planned, Lee ordered a retreat instead of fighting until Washington came to reinforce him.

When Washington discovered what was going on, he galloped forward furiously, gave Lee a severe tongue lashing in the presence of the men, and ordered him off the field in disgrace.

Thanks to von Steuben's training, Washington's men fought well. But Lee's disgraceful conduct had cost the Americans precious time. Clinton managed to take his army to New York.

At the Battle of Monmouth, Molly Pitcher earned her place in the history books. Her real name was Mary Hayes and she was the wife of John Hayes, one of Washington's cannoneers. At the start of the battle, she carried pitchers of fresh water to the soldiers in the fighting line. Then, when she saw her husband collapse at his gun, she dropped her pitcher and began to fire the cannon. She continued to keep the cannon firing until the battle was over.

The American Navy

The Revolutionary War was a land war in which America's midget sea power played only a minor role. The British Navy, at the outbreak of the war, was the mightiest in the world. For this reason, the British Armies had little trouble capturing and holding such seaports as New York, Charleston, and Savannah. And because Britain relied so heavily on her navy for delivering supplies, her inland troops like those at Saratoga found themselves constantly in danger of isolation from supply lines.

The most important segment of American power on the sea was her vast fleet of privateers. These privately-owned armed ships were little more than legalized pirates. Congress issued their owners "letters of marque" which gave them a legitimate right to prey on British merchant ships.

At one time or another, more than 2,000 of these privateers roamed the seas, all the way from the West Indies and the American coast, to Spain and the English Channel. When they came upon an unarmed merchantman, they put a prize crew aboard and sailed the captured ship into the nearest neutral port. Here, the cargo and the ship itself were sold, and the money divided between the owner, the captain, and the crews.

The battle between the "Bonhomme Richard" and the "Serapis."

36

Many wealthy American families today owe the beginnings of their fortunes to the fact that their ancestors owned or captained Revolutionary privateers.

Insofar as the privateers created a great deal of trouble for British merchant ships, and prevented supplies from being delivered to the English troops in America, they were an asset to the American cause. But sailors much preferred the easy life on a privateer and the easy money to be made from prizes to service with the little American Navy or the ground troops. To this extent, they were an evil.

Early in the war, Congress appropriated money for a small regular navy. Commodore Esek Hopkins was put in command. He was a daring man, although difficult for his superiors in Congress to get along with. His little squadrons inflicted much damage on British installations throughout the West Indies.

A few states had warships of their own. The most famous of these was the Massachusetts ship, *Protector*. While cruising off the Grand Banks, in June of 1780, she met the British ship, *Admiral Duff*. Both warships were about the same size, but the *Protector* was better served by her crew.

As the two ships came together, 60 American Marines scrambled to

COMMODORE ESEK HOPKINS

Cutaway view of a typical English warship, a 40-gun battleship of Revolutionary times. On the top story, from left to right, are the galley, the officers' quarters, the crews' quarters, the captain's sleeping quarters, the officers' mess, and the captain's cabin. On the lower decks are more crews' quarters, sail loft, magazine, sick bay, ship stores, and even a stable for horses.

the tops of her masts and proceeded to shoot down the crewmen in the Britishers' rigging, as well as the sailor at the helm. Meanwhile, the *Protector's* deck guns hammered at her enemy. The *Duff's* sails caught fire, and the flames quickly ran down to a powder magazine below decks. The *Duff* blew up and sank almost instantly.

When, in 1778, the French decided to come into the war as America's ally, the huge French fleet joined the side of the Yankees. The French were mainly interested in utilizing their naval power against the English in the West Indies and elsewhere. French warships did, however, transport large numbers of French soldiers to be added to Washington's army. At Yorktown, in the war's last battle, a French fleet defeated a smaller English fleet that had attempted to come to the aid of the British forces and thus contributed greatly to the final victory.

The most fabulous American ship of the war could hardly be called American at all except for the flag that flew at her masthead. She was an ex-French merchantman, her name was French, and her captain was a Scotsman. Her crew of 306 included 79 Americans and 137 French Marines. The remainder were Scotch, Irish, Scandinavians, and Portuguese. Yet she became one of the most famous ships in the story of American naval history.

She was the *Bonhomme Richard*, captained by John Paul Jones. The *Bonhomme Richard* was so old and her timbers so rotten that they could hardly support her guns. The guns themselves were antiquated and only barely serviceable. The spirit of her young skipper was the strongest thing about her.

On September 23, 1779, while cruising off the coast of England, Captain Jones sighted a convoy of British merchantmen under the guard of a big, brand-new British frigate, the *Serapis*. Jones at once moved in to attack, while the merchantmen fled for the safety of the shore.

In the first broadside, two of the *Richard's* big guns burst, killing their crews, and the rest of the battery had to be abandoned. Now Jones had only his smaller guns. Meanwhile, the heavy guns of the *Serapis* were pounding him to pieces. There was only one hope. By an amazing feat of seamanship, Jones managed to ram his decrepit old ship into the *Serapis'* side and lash it there. Most of the *Richard's* guns were out of action. Her rotten timbers caught fire repeatedly, and the flames were put out only by the Herculean efforts of the crew.

Seeing that the American ship was in the worst kind of trouble, the English captain called out through his speaking horn:

"Do you ask for quarter? Will you surrender?"

Jones yelled back with his now-famous remark: "I have not yet begun to fight!"

Then someone on the *Richard* threw a grenade into the *Serapis'* hold and exploded a store of ammunition. With a small cannon, Jones knocked off the Britisher's mast. The sun went down, and the furious battle continued in the moonlit night. Then the British captain surrendered. Jones and what was left of his crew had hardly stepped on board the *Serapis* when the battered old *Richard* sank, bow first. But as she went down, her flag was still proudly flying.

John Paul Jones managed to limp his captured prize into the port of Texel, Holland. There, because the Dutch were neutral, the authorities took the *Serapis* away from him.

The famous battle proved little, except that a brave man never quits. It did no material good to the American cause. But it gave Americans a glowing sense of pride that one of their ships could defeat a mighty unit of the British Navy. And it gave the British a new respect for the Americans' fighting ability. "Put to sea at once," the First Lord of the Admiralty implored one of his captains. "If you can take John Paul Jones, you will be as high in public esteem as if you had beaten the combined fleets of France and Spain."

Vincennes

Vincennes was a quiet little trading post and fort deep in the forests of what is now Indiana. Its people, mostly of French descent, were sympathetic to the cause of American independence, but they were far removed from the sound and fury of the war.

Then, on May 19, 1777, a British military unit from Detroit marched out of the woods and took possession of the fort in the King's name. Up until this time, the people of Vincennes were on friendly terms with the neighboring Indians. But now, since many of the Western tribes were allies of the British, Indian attacks on settlers outside the fort became common.

At this point, a major of the Virginia militia, named George Rogers Clark, went to Governor Patrick Henry with a bold plan to attack the garrison at Vincennes and chase the British out of the Northwest. The Governor agreed, and gave Clark men and supplies. After a grueling journey

MAJOR GEORGE ROGERS CLARK

Back to Vincennes through swamps and icy waters.

down the Ohio River and overland through rugged Indian country, Clark attacked the British garrison in August of 1778, and gave the town back to its people.

After Clark had organized the citizens of the town into a militia unit, he took his army back to Virginia. But he was gone only a few weeks when a second and larger British force, also from Detroit, captured Vincennes again. Now Clark had to redo all his work.

This time, weather conditions were infinitely worse than before. Winter rains and snows had flooded the entire countryside, and Clark's men had to make much of the 200-mile march, sloughing through icy waters that were sometimes up to their shoulders. But if the floods were a miserable hardship to the Americans, the major also knew that the weather gave him a decided strategic advantage. The British soldiers would be confined to the fort, and would not expect a surprise attack.

Clark and his wet and shivering men arrived in front of Vincennes on February 23, 1779, caught the British completely off their guard, and captured the fort without the loss of a single man. Clark then changed its name to Fort Patrick Henry.

By his bold action against the British at Vincennes, as well as at Kaskaskia and other Western forts, Clark managed to keep the Northwestern territory out of British hands and thus prevent an attack on the Eastern Colonies.

The Cherry Valley Massacre

Cherry Valley was a little outpost village in northeastern New York State. Because of its exposed position, the American Army had fortified it with a blockhouse the previous spring. It was garrisoned with a small force under the command of Colonel Ichabod Alden, a man who knew nothing about fighting Indians.

It has been pointed out that the chief value of the Indians to their British allies lay in harassing frontier settlements, and that they were of little help from a military standpoint. The Cherry Valley Massacre, on November 11, 1778, accomplished nothing for the British cause, but a good many helpless men, women, and children were cruelly and needlessly slain.

On November 8, a friendly Indian came in to the fort and warned the

colonel that a large force of Indians and American Loyalists were planning a raid on the town. But Colonel Alden did not take this information seriously.

Early in the morning of November 11, the raiding party, 800 strong, attacked the village. The white men were commanded by Captain Walter Butler, and the Indians by a half-breed Mohawk chief named Joseph Brant.

In the massacre that followed, 32 settlers, mostly women and children, were brutally killed, as well as Colonel Alden and 15 of his men. The raiders burned the town, the fort, and the surrounding farms to the ground, and carried off all the livestock they could get their hands on. In addition, 30 or 40 prisoners were taken, also mostly women and children. Later, most of the prisoners were returned in exchange for members of Captain Butler's family that were in American hands.

During what became known as the "Cherry Valley Massacre," Colonel Alden, 15 of his men, and 32 settlers were brutally killed.

41

The British Attack in the South

After the Battle of Monmouth, the last big engagement of the war in the North, the British changed their strategy. They decided to hold New York City, but send the bulk of their army south to attack the Carolinas and Virginia.

In the fall of 1779, a British Army of some 3,000 men set sail from New York for Savannah, Georgia. Only a handful of Americans were there to resist, and the city was captured almost without a fight. The Americans retreated into South Carolina, leaving Georgia in British hands.

The conquest of the South was beginning to look so easy after the many British defeats and disappointments in the North that Clinton determined to attack Charleston, the most important port in the Carolinas. This time he took a much larger army and General Cornwallis

Francis Marion, "the Swamp Fox," and his guerrilla forces became the terror of the British commanders.

Marion and his men (right) are about to ambush an enemy force.

as his second in command. In February of 1780, Clinton's huge army of 10,000 men surrounded the city.

The American forces in Charleston, commanded by General Benjamin Lincoln, found themselves in a hopeless position. Lincoln had less than half as many men as Clinton. Entirely surrounded, with all possible avenues of escape cut off and no chance of getting outside help, Lincoln had no choice but to surrender. His whole army, along with its guns, ammunition, and supplies fell into British hands. The American soldiers were released to go back to their homes on their promise never again to take up arms against the English King.

The British Army spread out and established posts all through the state. Clinton returned to New York, leaving Cornwallis in charge.

In the British Army, there were a great many Tories or Loyalists, as the Americans who remained loyal to the King were called. The sight of these fellow Americans strutting around proudly in redcoat uniforms was too much for the Carolina Militia Men who had been paroled at the Charleston surrender. Many Americans broke their oaths and joined parties of partisan raiders under leaders like the famous Francis Marion.

A gathering of the untrained mountaineers who dealt the well-trained British forces their first defeat in the South.

Known as the "Swamp Fox," Marion was one of the great leaders of the Revolution. He and his men made their headquarters in the swamps and woods, ambushing isolated parties of British soldiers and in general making themselves the terrors of the English commanders. His scouts kept close watch on all British movements, and dashed out to strike quick and telling blows when the enemy least expected them.

Meanwhile, before the Charleston surrender, Washington had sent an army under Generals Gates and de Kalb to assist Lincoln. When he received news of the surrender, Gates determined to continue on to Camden, South Carolina. When this army finally arrived at Camden after a long and weary march through the Southern woods and swamps, they found a British Army waiting for them. At the first British charge, Gates' inexperienced militia threw down their guns and took to their heels. Gates, who had the fastest horse in the army, fled ahead of them in panic. General de Kalb stayed to fight and to die from 11 bullet wounds.

Two American Armies had been lost in South Carolina, Lincoln's at Charleston, and Gates' at Camden. Aside from such irregulars as Marion's men, there were no more American fighters in the South.

Washington recalled Gates in disgrace, and appointed a man who was his best general, Nathaniel Greene, to reorganize the Southern forces.

A scene from the battle at Kings Mountain, where the Watauga Men put an end to Ferguson's forces.

MAJOR GENERAL
NATHANAEL GREENE

King's Mountain and Cowpens

An American Tory, Major Patrick Ferguson, had organized several thousand of his fellow Tories into a strong British Army in North Carolina. He used them to terrorize all that part of the South by raiding and burning rebel farms, and hanging people whom he suspected of being loyal Americans. As a result, Ferguson was widely hated.

One group that was a thorn in Ferguson's side was a band of patriotic frontiersmen from that part of the Watauga River which runs through the present state of Tennessee. They called themselves the Watauga Men, and were all dead shots with their long rifles. Wherever and whenever they could, these men resisted the British occupation. Ferguson declared that he was going across the mountains to teach the Watauga Men a lesson.

When they heard this, the Watauga Men made up their minds that they would hit Ferguson first. Accordingly, they marched through the forests and cornered Ferguson and his men at the top of Kings Mountain on the border between North and South Carolina.

All the Watauga sharpshooters climbed into trees, or fought from behind them, and picked off the Tories one by one, including Major Ferguson, himself.

At last, the remaining Tories, about 700 of them, surrendered. Having put an end to Ferguson's force, the Watauga Men went back home to their farms. Thus a band of untrained mountaineers were able to hand the well-trained British forces their first defeat in the South.

Nathanael Greene, sent by Washington to replace the cowardly Gates, moved south with a mere handful of poorly equipped men. Desperately needing time to reinforce and re-equip his little army, Greene took a chance and divided it into two parts. He commanded one, and Daniel Morgan, the famous leader of the riflemen, commanded the other. Then the two divisions went their separate ways.

Cornwallis sent Tarleton to deal with Morgan. They fought at a place called Cowpens in South Carolina. Morgan adopted the same tactics as had the Watauga Men at Kings Mountain. He stationed his sharpshooters in trees and behind logs, and was ready when Tarleton's army came on the scene.

Tarleton ordered a cavalry charge to dislodge the rebels, the worst possible move he could have made. The riflemen cooly shot the mounted targets. In the furious fight that followed, Tarleton lost 90 per cent of his men, but he himself managed to escape.

For the second time in the South, Americans fighting "Indian style" had annihilated trained British soldiers.

Yorktown

For the next four months, General Greene harassed Cornwallis all up and down North Carolina. Aside from one big battle at Guilford Courthouse that Cornwallis won, but in which he lost about one-fourth of his army, the engagements were small ones. Sometimes, the British were defeated; sometimes, the Americans. But the effect reduced Cornwallis' army to only a shell of what it had been in early spring.

Now the scene was set for the amazing and unexpected series of events that led to the final battle of the Revolutionary War and ultimate American victory. Cornwallis left the Carolinas and moved north to Virginia. There, he began a campaign of raiding and burning Virginia farms and storehouses.

Meanwhile, Washington had been keeping the main part of his army just outside of New York, waiting for a chance to strike at General Clinton who was maintaining a 15,000-man force within the city. But Washington's position seemed hopeless. At best, he had only 5,000 men, and his army's morale was almost at an all-time low. Soldiers were deserting in droves, and few, if any, new volunteers were coming forward.

At last, Washington began sending detachments under Lafayette, Anthony Wayne, and von Steuben down to Virginia to oppose Cornwallis' raiding tactics. Although the American Army in Virginia was gradually building up, Cornwallis' superior force continued to win whenever the Americans challenged them.

Cornwallis decided to build a permanent supply base in Virginia from which his army could operate. The little port of Yorktown, on Chesapeake Bay, seemed to be an ideal location. He took his army there in June and began at once to build fortifications.

While all this was going on, a huge French fleet started across the Atlantic, bringing with it several thousand French soldiers. Washington reluctantly gave up his plans to use these reinforcements against Clinton in New York, and decided, instead, to employ them against Cornwallis in Virginia. This decision, made against his better judgment, turned out to be the decisive one of the war. He left a small force in New York in order to fool Clinton into thinking that the bulk of his army was still there, and marched south with his main army. He was joined by 4,500 French regulars under General Rochambeau.

A British officer, waving a white flag and accompanied by a drummer boy, brought the message of surrender.

In September of 1781, Washington assembled his armies at Williamsburg, 14 miles from Yorktown. Almost as though by a miracle of timing and luck, Washington had, instead of the straggly army on which he had been forced to depend since the war's beginning, a combined American-French force of more than 15,000 men. The huge French fleet, having beaten a smaller English one and chased it back to New York, now commanded the entire bay. Cornwallis, with his army of 7,000, was caught in Yorktown in a trap he had fashioned himself.

Washington at once marched his army to Yorktown and laid siege to the fortifications. From all sides, French and American artillery blasted the British position with an almost 24-hour barrage. Cornwallis' supplies of food and ammunition began to run dangerously low. His men were worn out by sickness and the fatigue of the unending bombardment. Only a few thousand were fit enough to man the defense works. At one point, Cornwallis made a desperate attempt to escape, but he failed.

There was nothing Cornwallis could do. On October 17, a British officer waving a white flag, and accompanied by a drummer, appeared on top of the fortifications and signaled for a parley. He had a message from the general. Cornwallis wanted to surrender.

Two days later, the British Army marched out of Yorktown to the blaring of their own bands, passed between lines of Frenchmen and Americans, and laid down their arms.

At that very moment, Clinton, with 7,000 men, was on his way to reinforce Cornwallis. But when his fleet arrived off Chesapeake Bay, it was all over. He sailed back to New York.

The conditions of the surrender were in the same terms as those imposed on General Lincoln at the surrender of Charleston. Lincoln was given the honor of overseeing the laying down of arms and the disposal of prisoners.

No one thought that the surrender of Yorktown was the end of the war, least of all, George Washington. Anxious to take advantage of the splendid forces that had been assembled here for the siege, he tried to persuade the French commanders to join with him in the conquest of New York. But Rochambeau decided to keep his army in Virginia, and the admiral of the French fleet took his ships and troops on to the West Indies. Washington then took his Americans and marched northward to the Hudson.

Independence at Last

Yorktown was the last straw. The British had had enough. The King stubbornly wanted to keep on fighting but his ministers demanded that the futile war be ended. It was now apparent that the American Colonies could never be subdued.

Besides, the British Parliament had plenty of other headaches. England was still at war with France and Spain, and soldiers were desperately needed in the West Indies, Africa, and Gibraltar. If the more than 30,000 men stationed in New York, Charleston, and Savannah could quickly be sent to the West Indies, for example, it might mean a British victory in those islands.

Furthermore, the war had continued for longer than anyone had imagined possible. The British war debt was mounting. Taxes in England were alarmingly high, and the King's treasury was practically bankrupt. Thus, the English Armies were removed from America as rapidly as possible.

Washington disbanded his army and went to live in peace on his Mount Vernon plantation. He intended to remain there for the rest of his life, never dreaming that he would be called back to serve his country again as its first President.

On September 3, 1783, Britain signed the Treaty of Paris, recognizing the United States of America as an independent nation.

With the war over at last, Americans hung up their guns, rolled up their sleeves, and went to work to build a new country — a country that one day would become the spiritual leader of all freedom-loving men the world over.

General Benjamin Lincoln, who had suffered the shame of surrender at Charleston, was honored by General Washington with the distinction of receiving General O'Hara's sword as a sign of the surrender of Cornwallis.

Highlights of the Revolutionary War

1765

Oct. 7-25   Stamp Act Congress meets in New York. Sends memorandum to the King and Parliament. Adopts Declaration of Rights and Liberties.

1766

March 17   Stamp Act repealed.

1770

March 5   The Boston Massacre. British troops fire on citizens, killing and wounding several.

1773

Dec. 16   The Boston Tea Party. Parliament orders port closed, sends four regiments to Boston.

1774

Sept. 5-Oct. 26   First Continental Congress meets at Philadelphia.

1775

March 23   Patrick Henry addresses Revolutionary convention at Richmond, ending, "Give me liberty or give me death!"

April 18   Paul Revere and William Dawes ride to rouse the Minute Men to meet British forces on way to destroy stores at Concord, Mass.

April 19   British meet Minute Men at the Battle of Lexington, press on to Concord, but are pushed back to Lexington and Boston.

May 10-12   Ticonderoga captured by Ethan Allen and Benedict Arnold. Seth Warner captures Crown Point.

June 15   George Washington named Commander in Chief by Continental Congress.

June 17   British are victorious in Battle of Bunker Hill under Gen. William Howe, but suffer heavy losses.

July 3   Washington takes command at Cambridge, Mass., in siege of Boston.

Nov. 13   Montreal captured by American forces under Richard Montgomery.

Dec. 30-31   Quebec assaulted; Montgomery killed.

1776

March 4   Washington occupies Dorchester Heights outside Boston.

March 17   British evacuate Boston.

May 15   Virginia Convention instructs its delegates to urge Congress to declare independence.

June 7   Resolution for independence offered in Continental Congress by Richard Henry Lee of Virginia.

July 2   Lee's resolution adopted.

July 4   Declaration of Independence adopted.

Aug. 27   Colonials defeated in Battle of Long Island, retreat to New York.

Sept. 15   Washington retreats to Harlem Heights; New York is occupied.

Sept. 16   Battle of Harlem Heights; Washington retreats to White Plains.

Sept. 22   Nathan Hale executed as spy by British.

Oct. 11   Lake Champlain fleet under Arnold defeated at Valcour Island.

Oct. 28   Washington's forces survive attack at White Plains but are forced to retreat.

Nov. 16-20   Ft. Washington in Manhattan and Ft. Lee, N. J., fall to the Hessians.

Dec. 25-26   Washington crosses the Delaware River; Hessians defeated in the Battle of Trenton.

1777

Jan. 3   Battle of Princeton. Lord Cornwallis defeated by Washington.

June 14   Stars and Stripes voted official flag by Continental Congress.

June 27   Ft. Ticonderoga taken by British under Maj. Gen. John Burgoyne.

Aug. 16   Battle of Bennington (Vt.) won by the Green Mountain Boys.

Sept. 11   Battle of Brandywine Creek. Washington defeated at Chad's Ford.

Sept. 19   British attack American encampment at Bemis Heights, N. Y. At Freeman's Farm, British are beaten back with severe losses.

Sept. 27   British occupy Philadelphia; Congress flees to Lancaster.

Oct. 4   Washington defeated in Battle of Germantown (Pa.); settles in for winter at Valley Forge.

Oct. 6   British seize Fts. Clinton and Montgomery near West Point.

Oct. 7   Burgoyne repulsed at Bemis Heights, and escape route of British is closed.

Oct. 17   Burgoyne surrenders at Saratoga.

Nov. 15   Continental Congress adopts Articles of Confederation and Perpetual Union, giving name of United States of America to the confederacy.

1778

Feb. 6   France recognizes American independence, signs treaties of alliance and commerce with delegation headed by Benjamin Franklin. French fleet dispatched under Admiral Jean Baptiste d'Estaing.

June 18   British evacuate Philadelphia.

June 28   Washington is victorious at Battle of Monmouth.

July 4   Indian massacre at Wyoming, Pa.

July 8   French fleet arrives off Delaware, plans attack on British at Newport to be coordinated with land attack by Washington.

Aug. 9   Storm at sea damages French fleet, causing abandonment of planned attack. Gen. John Sullivan left unsupported when D'Estaing proceeds to Boston for repairs.

Aug. 29   Sullivan drops siege of Newport.

Nov. 11   Indian massacre at Cherry Valley, N. Y. 32 settlers and 16 American soldiers slain.

Dec. 29   British capture Savannah.

1779

Feb. 23   Major George Rogers Clark captures the fort at Vincennes, Ind., completing the conquest of the Northwest Territory. (He had earlier (1778) taken Cahokia and Kaskaskia in Illinois.)

July 15   Gen. Anthony ("Mad Anthony") Wayne assaults Stony Point on the Hudson River but withdraws after winning.

Sept. 23   John Paul Jones is victor in sea battle of the *Bonhomme Richard* against the *Serapis* and *Countess of Scarborough*.

1780

May 12   Colonials surrender Charleston, S. C.

Aug. 16   General Horatio Gates is defeated by Lord Cornwallis at Battle of Camden, S. C.

Sept. 23   Major John André captured, found to be carrying papers incriminating Benedict Arnold in a plot to betray West Point. Arnold escapes and joins British.

Oct. 2   Major André hanged as a spy.

Oct. 7   British defeated in Battle of Kings Mountain, N. C.

1781

Jan. 17   British cavalry defeated in Battle of Cowpens, S. C.

March 15   British gain in Battle of Guilford Courthouse, N. C., but Cornwallis is driven to retreat to Wilmington, N. C., by action of

Maj. Gen. Nathanael Greene. Cornwallis later withdraws to Yorktown, Va.

Sept. 8   British defeated in Battle of Eutaw Springs, S. C., withdraw to Charleston, W. Va.

Sept. 30   Siege of Yorktown begins, Cornwallis bottled up by American and French forces.

Oct. 19   Cornwallis surrenders.

1783

Sept. 3   Peace treaty between the U.S. and Britain signed in Paris, France.

THE WAR BETWEEN THE STATES

Our Country a Hundred Years Ago

Our country, 100 years ago, was like a growing boy or girl whose arms, legs, head, and body sometimes acted as though they were strangers. As a nation, we were still painfully, awkwardly young. Only 71 years before, George Washington had been elected first President of 13 states that, "with tongue in cheek," had agreed to try living together under a government elected by the people.

Yet we had done better than anybody had expected. We were now a nation of 34 states and our flag proudly spanked in the breeze upon the shores of the blue Pacific. Along the rivers and through the mountain passes that hardy frontiersmen had followed to discover a vast continent, we had begun to build railroads and highways. Across still unsettled territories where wild animals and hostile Indians roamed, Pony Express riders carried the mail between East and West. Proud steamboats churned the Mississippi, and adventuresome homesteaders broke the hard sod of Kansas with their crude wooden plows, and along the Texas border a colonel named Robert E. Lee chased Indians, and across the undeveloped West men strung the wires of the new-fangled telegraph.

So, as one country, we were beginning to come together, but we were only beginning. America a hundred years ago remained pretty much what you saw with your own eyes and heard with your own ears.

For example, since in New England there were many falls in the rivers that could supply cheap power, it was logical to build factories and the New England boy and girl grew up in an America where people held jobs making products and shipping them to the markets of the world.

For another example, since the land in the South was suitable for growing cotton, plantations cultivated by slaves had developed as a natural way of life, and Southern boys and girls were taught to accept slaves with kindness and understanding as their rightful property.

A third class of Americans, restless and ambitious, moved into the undeveloped territories seeking a new start in life. If they came from the South they brought Southern ideas, and if they came from New England they brought New England ideas. Both believed that they were normal, decent fellows at heart, and since they had the gumption to push out on their own, they didn't much like to be shoved around by anyone.

It was a wonderful country, really — full of life and rich with promise.

Proud steamboats churned the Mississippi and other American waterways.

Already it had developed great cities — New York, Philadelphia, Baltimore, Boston, Cincinnati, Louisville, and that booming young upstart on the shores of Lake Michigan, Chicago. From all the countries of Europe people came to America, seeking freedom and a new life. St. Louis, a city of red brick houses on the banks of the Mississippi, was a good example of what such migrations could mean. From fifty to sixty thousand Germans now lived in St. Louis — loyal Americans to the core who in another year would march off to war.

It was a go-ahead, pick-yourself-up-by-the-bootstraps country. Gold in the Rockies, gold in the Sierra Nevada — nobody knew how rich the land might be. It was a country that could grow corn and wheat and graze great herds of cattle, a country of unbelievable beauty to make a lump come into your throat, a country where people worked hard and played hard and on Sunday put on their best clothes and went to church morning, noon, and night. Its folk heroes were Johnny Appleseed planting his orchards in the wilderness and Paul Bunyan creating another lake wherever he stepped and Mike Fink spinning his yarns and fighting with the other keel boatmen of the Ohio.

The country 100 years ago was still largely unsettled. It was a giant, waking up, and now and then finding a hen that could lay a golden egg. People awoke in the morning to a sense of adventure just around the

Homestead laws made possible the settlement of public lands in Kansas and other territories.

Colonel Robert E. Lee fought off Indians along the Texas border in the days before the Civil War.

Europeans and Americans came to the unsettled country of the open West.

corner — an Indian raid maybe, or a new gold strike, or the never-failing excitement of a steamboat coming round the bend.

And yet it was a troubled country. Growth brought problems — people who began wondering if what they heard in church on Sunday they practiced on Monday, and if the old ways were necessarily the best ways, and if with all the angry talking that was going on there wouldn't be some angry fighting sooner or later.

In time, of course, there was a lot of fighting, and this is the story of how it came about—and why—and how it all turned out—and again why.

The Gathering Storm

A Connecticut Yankee was really at the bottom of all the trouble that developed, although this fact wasn't his fault. When, 71 years before, Washington had become our first President, we had believed that slavery would soon die out. For a number of years, societies working to free the slaves were far more numerous in the South than in the North. But then along came that Connecticut Yankee — Eli Whitney — who invented a machine for separating cotton from its seed. With Whitney's "cotton gin" a crop could be harvested more quickly and with much higher profits,

Southern boys organized into military units, taking such names as the "Cherokee Lincoln Killers" to make absolutely clear where they stood in the critical situation.

and when in England at about this time machinery was invented for spinning fine cotton thread, the South could sell all the cotton it could grow.

The South soon forgot it ever had wanted to free its slaves. Indeed, argued those who needed slaves to grow more and more cotton, look at how well we use the Negro. When he is sick or too old to work, we care for him. Now, in contrast, take your white "wage slave" in New England and let him grow ill or old and what happens? You kick him out to starve!

But the torment of mind and heart that once had haunted even the South lived on. Slavery was not right. No man should be another man's master or live by the sweat of another man's brow. In the North and in a large part of the booming Midwest, where slaves were not needed (nor wanted), the movement to end slavery grew enormously.

For a long time, the statesmen of the nation tried to keep this great conflict of mind and heart within check. Whenever a "slave" state was admitted to the Union, a "free" state was also admitted. Boundaries were set beyond which, we said, slavery could not pass.

The nation kept growing, however. Like steam in a boiler, the pressure mounted to sweep aside such restrictions and tempers broke under the heat of this pressure. Northerners who opposed slavery were called troublemakers, stealers of slaves, tyrants who wanted to rule the country.

In Kansas, open warfare broke out between those who supported and those who opposed slavery as the territory organized for admission to the Union. And in Illinois, a strong voice spoke up, warning the nation: "We cannot be half slave and half free." The voice belonged to Abraham Lincoln.

In the election of 1860, the people came face to face with a decision. Two Democrats ran for President — Stephen A. Douglas of Illinois, who said that it was up to the settlers of a territory to decide whether they wished to be a slave state or a free state, and John C. Breckinridge of Kentucky, who believed that no territory had a right to forbid slavery. As the Republican candidate, Lincoln said he would not interfere with slavery where it then existed but it should extend no further. The Union Party candidate, John Bell of Tennessee, ignored the issue of slavery.

The two Democratic candidates drew a total popular vote of 2,226,738 against 1,866,452 for Lincoln, but Lincoln amassed 180 Electoral votes against their 84 — a smashing victory. Quickly, the supporters of slavery reacted. No "Black Republican" was going to tell the South how it must live! Military companies began to form, taking such names as the "Cherokee Lincoln Killers" to make absolutely clear where they stood. Nobody really wanted war. But war was what the nation faced.

In 1860, after a hard-fought campaign, Abe Lincoln was elected the 16th President of the United States.

Six Critical Weeks

The South moved swiftly to break with the Union and establish its own government. Amid the tolling of church bells and the joyous shouts of people, South Carolina seceded on December 22, 1860, and by early February six other states had followed its example — Georgia, Mississippi, Alabama, Florida, Louisiana, and Texas. In Montgomery, Alabama, delegates from these states met that month to form the Confederate States of America and to write a constitution that recognized slaves as property. For President, they selected Jefferson Davis, a stanch states-righter from Mississippi, and except for Fort Sumter in Charleston Harbor, Fort Pickens in Pensacola Bay, and two small forts off the Florida coast, all Federal establishments were seized in the seceding states.

Montgomery, the capital of the new nation, went wild with excitement. Think of it! Without shedding a drop of blood — and even before Old Abe Lincoln had reached Washington — Southern independence had been achieved! But one thorn still stung Southern pride. On Christmas night in Charleston Harbor, a small Federal force under Major Robert Anderson had moved unexpectedly from antiquated Fort Moultrie (which was impossible to defend) to Fort Sumter (which only could be approached by water and which controlled the sea lanes into the harbor). An insult, raged the South. A symbol of national honor, replied the North.

Lincoln, traveling from his home in Springfield, Illinois, to become President of a now-divided nation, tried to appear undisturbed by the impending crisis. From one whistle stop to the next, he struck the same theme: "We are not enemies, but friends." Given time to think through the problem, he believed Americans would respond to "the better angels" of their spirits. Born in Kentucky, grown to manhood in Indiana, matured on the prairies of Illinois, he had a sublime faith in the strength of the nation — and in the hard, good sense of the common people. It was clear that Lincoln would not back down on one principle. In Indianapolis he asked: "What is the peculiar sacredness of a state?" At any cost, the Union must be held together!

On March 4, 1861, tenseness lay over crowded Washington, D. C. At noon, the retiring President, James Buchanan, called at Willard's Hotel to escort Lincoln to the ceremonies that would make him the 16th President. Old Winfield Scott, the General of the Army, was worried sick over the many threats that had been made against Lincoln's life — threats like the one from a correspondent called "Vindex" who informed Lincoln that "a sworn Band of 10" had resolved "to shoot you from the south side of the Avenue in the inaugural procession."

General Scott took no chances. Soldiers stood on rooftops and at street crossings to guard against possible assassins. Expert marksmen were stationed at each window where the wings of the Capitol flanked the inaugural stand. Lincoln, wearing a new black suit, arose erect and unruffled, and spoke from his heart. "One section of our country believes slavery is *right*, and ought to be extended," he said, "while the other believes it is *wrong*, and ought not to be extended. This is the only substantial dispute."

But trouble a-plenty awaited Lincoln. Provisions were running low at Fort Sumter and its small Federal garrison would soon be starved out unless supplies were delivered. Six critical weeks followed with each day filled with mounting war talk. The Secretary of State, William H. Seward, speaking off the record, assured Confederate commissioners in Washington that Sumter would be abandoned. Meanwhile, Colonel Robert E. Lee was offered field command of the Northern forces should war come, but he declined. Lee would fight only in defense of his beloved Virginia, yet he did not deny that he hated slavery.

"If I owned four million slaves," Lee told a friend, "I would cheerfully sacrifice them for the preservation of the Union."

Despite threats on his life, Lincoln took the oath of office.

Seward's promise that Sumter would be abandoned was not fulfilled, and Southern patience neared the breaking point. Both Virginia and Missouri voted against immediate secession, proof that if Lincoln was allowed enough time to stall on the Sumter crisis, the Confederacy might collapse under its own weight. In Charleston, the "hot-heads" screamed for action. But Lincoln could delay no longer. He must attempt to provision Sumter, and so the South learned that Federal ships were at sea for that very purpose. Orders were sent to General Pierre Gustave Toutant Beauregard, commanding the Confederate forces in Charleston. "Demand at once the surrender of the fort," those orders instructed. And if the demand were refused? In that event, the orders continued, ". . . proceed in such a manner as you may determine, to reduce it."

War Over a Fort

The demand was refused. And so, at 4:30 on the morning of April 12, 1861, a single mortar boomed out in Charleston Harbor. Many eyes followed the burning fuse of the shell as it arched among the twinkling stars. For a moment, it seemed to hang suspended in the night sky, then faster and faster the shell descended. It struck with a flash inside the fort, bursting into a hundred fragments.

To save ammunition, the Federal forces waited until daylight to return the fire, and then only an occasional shell was thrown into the city. Through the day, as the uneven duel went on, jubilant Charlestonians crowded rooftops and cheered their cannoneers with each new burst of flame within the fort.

With the shelling of Fort Sumter, which the Union surrendered, the War Between the States began. The fort is now a United States monument.

A Federal gunner in Sumter, beholding this throng, growled to a mate: "If it's war they like, then 'tis war they shall get!" He aimed a 42-pounder at the spectators and let fly. The shot bounded 50 yards above the heads of the onlookers and they were soon scampering for cover.

But this was a small triumph at best for the beleaguered Union forces, who were pounded mercilessly by the Confederate gunners. As the day wore on, the skies darkened and strong winds began to blow. Soon waves were splashing high against the walls of the old fort, bringing a new anxiety. Even though Federal ships were standing off the bar of the harbor, waiting for nightfall to bring supplies so desperately needed, how could they land in a sea like this?

Night arrived, and the winds now were almost a gale. The Carolinians had begun to use red-hot shot, a new menace. Fires broke out everywhere. Suppose one of these incendiary shells struck the powder magazine? In the wink of an eye, every man in the fort could be blown to bits!

Only the tiniest portion of pork fat remained next morning to feed the famished, bone-weary gunners in Sumter. Still, the fires raged. Still, the seas rolled in great waves against dock and pilings. Still, the Confederate shells rained down on the fort.

At last Major Anderson accepted the grim truth — he must surrender. Fifty guns roared out in salute to the Stars and Stripes when, the following day, Anderson and his men proudly marched out of Sumter.

Already newsboys were racing through the streets of Northern cities, shouting a single headline:

"War! War! War!"

Patriotism

All work stopped in those cities. People gathered to read the latest bulletins. Stunned and bewildered at first, a seething anger rose in their hearts. By the rockets' red glare, the glorious old flag of the Union had been "insulted." The Philadelphia *Press* wrote editorially: "Henceforth each man, high and low, must take his position as a patriot or a traitor — as a foe or friend of his country — as a supporter of the Stars and Stripes or of the rebel banner."

Patriotism swept like a tidal wave across the North. That Sunday, practically every church steeple flew the national flag. Next day, President Lincoln called for 75,000 state militia men to serve in the national armies for three months and the response was immediate and overwhelming. Men rushed to join military companies, and quickly they embarked to guard Washington from the attack that everyone expected to come at almost any moment. The Governor of Massachusetts spoke the general feeling when he addressed a company of volunteers about to board a steamer:

"You have come from the shores of the sounding sea, where lie the ashes of the Pilgrims, and you are bound on a high and noble pilgrimage for liberty, and for the Union and Constitution of your country."

The determination of the North to stand by the Union was shrugged off in the South with boasts that one Confederate could lick ten Yankees! And Southern politicians, echoing an old chant, shouted: "Cotton is King!" How long, they asked, would foreign powers like Great Britain stand idly by if the North interfered with the South's cotton trade?

Others pursued another argument. How, really, did Southern independence change the normal way of life in the North? Once Northerners realized this fact, and thus came to their senses, how long could Lincoln sustain the wave of war hysteria now sweeping the North? All these were good questions for bolstering Southern morale, but they contained one danger. Suppose the South was wrong and the North went on fighting? Then in time the North must win, for it possessed more of everything with which to fight a war — more people, money, raw materials, factories, food, railroads, ships.

Yet Lincoln also was faced with troublesome "if's." A week after the guns at Charleston had plunged the nation into civil war, troops of the Sixth Massachusetts Volunteers reached Baltimore where they were forced to change trains for Washington. Baltimore claimed many Southern sympathizers who reacted violently to this "invasion" of Maryland's soil. In an ugly mood, they barricaded the trolley route between railroad stations.

The sight of the Union soldiers was greeted by derisive catcalls.

Many cried, "Hurrah for Jeff Davis," and the cheers grew thunderous when a fellow appeared carrying a Confederate flag. Thus emboldened, the mob followed verbal taunts with a shower of brickbats. In exasperation, the Massachusetts troops fired at their tormentors and a shocked nation next morning read the grim score of the Baltimore riot — four soldiers dead, twelve civilians killed.

In New Orleans, a school teacher who had spent happy boyhood years in Baltimore could scarcely sleep as news of the riot set his mind afire with a poem. His name was James Ryder Randall and he deserves to be remembered, for his poem, set to music, became one of the great patriotic songs rallying the South to war:

> *"The despot's heel is on thy shore,*
> > *Maryland!*
> *His torch is at thy temple door,*
> > *Maryland!*
> *Avenge the patriotic gore*
> > *That flecked the streets of Baltimore,*
> *And be the battle-queen of yore,*
> > *Maryland, my Maryland!"*

Despite the tremendous ardor for the Southern cause that "Maryland, My Maryland" expressed, Lincoln managed to keep this border state from leaving the Union. Virginia was another story. Quickly, after Sumter, the Old Dominion State joined the Confederacy, and with her went the general the North had wanted — Robert E. Lee.

Meanwhile, both North and South, the people clamored for one great pitched battle that would end the war. Nobody then would listen to Lee, who was saying: "This war may last ten years." So, in hot July, at Manassas Junction, Virginia, the public had its way against the advice of sound military men like Generals Robert E. Lee and Winfield Scott. It learned a lesson that took years to forget.

Amateurs at War

North Carolina and Tennessee by now had followed Virginia into the Confederacy, and the Rebel capital had been moved from Montgomery to Richmond, Virginia. The North took up a new cry — "On to Richmond!" — but that remained a hollow threat as long as a great Confederate army under General Beauregard, the hero of Sumter, was stationed at Manassas Junction. Indeed, the advance guard of these Southern troops was at Fairfax Court House, practically within sight of the Federal capital, so that "On to Washington!" seemed even more logical.

Chock-full of confidence and fight, the Union boys on July 15, 1861, marched into Virginia, determined to oust these Rebels from the doorway to Washington. Green as young apples at war, the Union lads moved off to battle as though going on a picnic. They stopped to pick blackberries. They joked and ambled along and blocked the roads over which supply wagons and artillery caissons were trying to move. To add to the confusion, Congressmen in fancy carriages rode out from Washington "to see the show" — everyone in the North, it appeared, believed that war was something like a baseball game.

After three days, the Union troops reached a little stream called Bull Run. Here they met their first Rebels — a handful of advance pickets — who exchanged a few shots and fell back, but the great pitched battle that everyone wanted quickly developed. A redheaded colonel who later would win fame — his name was William Tecumseh Sherman — never forgot this experience "when for the first time in my life I saw cannonballs strike men and crash through trees above and around us, and realized the always sickening confusion as one approaches a fight from the rear." And Sherman remembered also "the terrible scare of a poor Negro who was caught between our lines."

Truly, the Battle of Manassas (called the Battle of Bull Run in Northern accounts) was a strange conflict. Each contending commander — Beauregard for the South and Irvin McDowell for the North — tried to

Stuart attacked the Zouaves at Manassas (the Battle of Bull Run).

swing his army around the other's right flank. Now, suppose this strategy had worked, for then, unopposed, the Northern forces would have been facing Richmond and, equally unopposed, the Southern forces would have been facing Washington!

But battles rarely go according to plan. At first, the Union boys seemed to have the Rebels on the run. They rolled up a hill by the Henry House, but there met bitter opposition from Confederate General Jackson, who, an admirer said, stood "like a stone wall," and who ever after would be known in history as the immortal Stonewall Jackson. Even so, the Federal troops kept pushing hard while the Confederate lines sagged more and more dangerously, and toward mid-afternoon a great Union victory appeared in the making. But at that critical moment a second Southern army under General Joseph E. Johnston reached the field.

These reinforcements proved too much for the Union boys. All at once the battle was going the *other* way — and then it became a panic, with Federal generals, soldiers, and Congressmen scampering like scared rabbits back to Washington. Had the Rebels pursued them vigorously, nobody knows what might have happened, but at this point the Rebs also were as green as young apples at war!

North and South, sober people read the terrible result of this battle that really had decided nothing. The Union forces at Manassas had numbered 28,452, and now 481 were dead, 1,011 were wounded, and 1,216 were missing either as deserters or prisoners. The Confederate forces had numbered 32,232, and now 387 were dead, 1,582 wounded, and 12 missing. But grim reading though these figures made, the bitterest part of the story was between the lines in the truth left unspoken, and which now so many people realized. This brothers' quarrel, before it ended, was likely to be long, bloody, and costly.

How many battles, skirmishes, and raids it took finally to end this war nobody can say for certain, but 10,000 is a fairly safe guess.

Quickly, the war spread until it touched America from the Texas border to a Vermont town only 15 miles from Canada. No hamlet along the Atlantic Seacoast was safe and in the wilderness of far-off Minnesota, the Sioux Indians staged a bloody uprising that Federal troops had to quell.

As the anger of the brothers deepened, and they began to fight for keeps, the war touched every ocean.

After Sumter, almost everyone had believed that the conflict could be ended in 90 days. Instead, as later events would demonstrate, America had plunged headlong into the bloodiest civil war the world ever had known!

On the Seas

When on April 19, 1861, Lincoln declared a blockade of the coast-line of all the seceding states, some Southerners almost split their sides with laughter.

That big clown Lincoln — whom did he think he was bluffing? Why, there were only three warships in Northern ports ready for action! And just suppose all 90 ships in the Union Navy were reconditioned — how did Lincoln think he was going to patrol 3,549 miles of Atlantic coast and seal off 180 Southern ports? And how about the old Mississippi — with its tributaries, Old Mis' added 3,615 miles for Lincoln's boats to patrol. Then there were sounds, bayous, and rivers emptying into the Atlantic — *and* the coast of the Gulf of Mexico — in round figures, another 2,000 miles!

But Lincoln wasn't bluffing. Perhaps the President's greatest strength was the fact that he was neither the dummy nor the insincere tyrant the South was forever calling him. Rather, he was the man with a good head above his bony shoulders who possessed the heart of a lion and the tenacity of a bearcat. Take, for example, what he achieved with the Union Navy. Maybe it had only 90 ships in 1861, but four years later it claimed 670! During the same period, its number of officers jumped from 1,300 to 6,700 and its seamen from 7,500 to 51,500. In 1861, the Federal Government was spending $12,000,000 a year to support its navy and by 1865, it had hiked that figure to $123,000,000!

Ultimately, the South stopped laughing about Lincoln's blockade, for it was both real and dangerous. Then, alert, in trouble, the South struck back with its fleet of blockade runners. Men seeking quick, rich profits sailed these vessels under the nose of the Federal patrol in one of the most rousing series of adventures of the sea that the war produced.

For a moment, think of yourself as a blockade runner. You have taken a load of cotton to one of four ports — Nassau, Bermuda, Havana, or Matamoros — and in exchange, have picked up a cargo of medicine. Now you've got to get back to a port in Georgia, and you must reckon accurately. On the average, that journey will consume three days. You consider weather and tides, for both mean life and death to you.

You're lucky — you've guessed right — and you approach the Georgian coast on a moonless night with the tide running high. You black out your ship, and cover binnacle and fireroom hatch.

"Blow off that steam underwater," you order severely, for off in that darkness — somewhere, anywhere — is the dragnet of Yankee patrol boats. Heart in throat, you drift with the tide — fingers crossed, praying hard.

Tense moments tick by. Off in the distance, you hear voices — lookouts on a Federal ship changing watch. Boy, you're really praying now!

Did you make it?

Making Naval History

In February, 1862, Lincoln and his Cabinet had reason to feel as worried sick as they clearly were.

The source of their sleepless nights was the fact that when the Federal troops had left the Gosport Navy Yard at Norfolk, Virginia, they hadn't done a good job. They had been ordered to destroy the *Merrimack*, one of the finest warships in the United States Navy, but the Confederates had put out the fire and now owned this magnificent ship. Moreover, as Lincoln and his Cabinet had learned to their distress, the Rebs were raising a slanting, ironplated superstructure on the vessel's berth deck. Low and ugly, the *Merrimack* was being converted into a new kind of fighting ship designed to blow the North's wooden battlewagons from the seas!

Against this threat, the North was gambling on what seemed like a pitiful experiment — John Ericsson's odd-shaped *Monitor* with its flat deck and squat, revolving gun turret so that it looked like "a cheese box on a raft." Some said that if the *Monitor* fought the *Merrimack*, it would be like sending a pygmy to fight with a giant.

Faces in Washington grew longer and gloomier than dark shoelaces when, on the afternoon of March 8, 1862, the *Merrimack* appeared off Hampton Roads, Virginia, flying the black flag she intended as the symbol of death to the North's wooden navy! What hours of despair followed for the Union as the ironclad *Merrimack* struck at the Federal vessels! The mighty *Cumberland* went down in flames. The *Congress* grounded in the mud and burned. The *Minnesota* also grounded, but nightfall saved her — that is, until daylight when the *Merrimack* would surely come back to finish her work of rewriting naval history.

Officials in Washington shivered in their boots, as though expecting at any moment to have the *Merrimack* come churning up the Potomac and lay waste to the national capital. But next morning, the *Merrimack*

The greatest naval battle of the war took place between the South's "Merrimack" and the Union's "Monitor," a duel won by the "Monitor."

was again off Hampton Roads. Then, suddenly, "a little black mass" appeared — the *Monitor*. On came Ericsson's queer vessel.

It was difficult for those who watched that famous sea battle to believe what they saw. Broadside after broadside fired by the *Merrimack* seemed only to bounce off the *Monitor* until in despair, one Southerner admitted the truth: "It's like so many pebblestones thrown by a child!" Meanwhile, the *Monitor* was far from idle. Her turret spun around and dropped open a port cover. Out popped an 11-inch gun. Boom! The gun sprang back. The port cover slammed shut. There was nothing to hit!

Through the morning the pygmy dueled the giant, and at last, badly sagging, the *Merrimack* limped back to Norfolk. The North cheered the *Monitor*, and soon men were smoking cigars named "El Monitor"! Great Britain suddenly looked with respect at the Federal Navy, for she hadn't a first-class ship that could stand against Ericsson's spunky little freak.

Professionals at War

Like a dog cooling its nose, a strip of Virginia between the York and James Rivers rests in the waters of Chesapeake Bay. Called the Peninsula, this strip of land in 1862 provided a natural highway to Richmond and the heart of the Confederacy.

Traveling up the Peninsula was like journeying through the pages of American history! At Yorktown stood the battleground where George Washington had won a decisive victory over the British redcoats under Lord Cornwallis. In Williamsburg were streets that once had echoed with the footsteps of Thomas Jefferson and Patrick Henry.

In all America there was not more sacred ground, and along roads that Washington once had ridden, a Federal Army of 110,000 under General George B. McClellan drove toward Richmond in the spring of 1862.

General McClellan's Army of the Potomac was the greatest fighting organization ever assembled on the American continent. Whenever it moved, the effect was the same as though a city like Albany or Indianapolis, with all its people, horses, wagons, food, and ambulances, had moved. It even carried balloons with which to send soldiers into the sky to spy on the enemy.

McClellan was no amateur at war. Trained at West Point, he already

Artillery was dragged through swampland near Yorktown.

had won a victory for the North in the mountains of western Virginia and his soldiers believed in him. But he was slow and cautious and confused, believing reports that the Confederates opposing him were at least twice as strong as they actually were. He distrusted Lincoln, with whom he bickered constantly. Still, mile by mile, McClellan ground his way up the Peninsula until the sound of his guns was distinctly heard in Richmond.

Robert E. Lee, who served an inconspicuous role in the war as a military advisor to Jefferson Davis, watched in agony this slow advance of the Union troops. Confederate forces on the Peninsula were under the command of Joseph E. Johnston, who had saved Beauregard in the battle at Manassas Junction, but now Johnston kept falling back on Richmond without offering a firm stand against McClellan. Where, when, Lee asked anxiously, was Johnston's retreat to stop? At a meeting of the Confederate Cabinet, Lee spoke with tears running down his cheeks:

"Richmond must not be given up — it shall not be given up!"

Yet McClellan was in trouble. Heavy rains endangered the Union's bridges across the Chickahominy River, and finally on May 31, 1862, Johnston was persuaded to strike an exposed flank of McClellan's army. The vicious Battle of Seven Pines that resulted seemed to decide little, but its impact upon the war was enormous since Johnston was wounded and the supreme command of the Confederate forces passed to Lee.

The South had found its man of history and of legend — the immortal Lee, who would live forever as the heroic symbol of the South. In character, Lee went to work almost around the clock. He suspected that the right wing of McClellan's army was "in the air" — that is, unsupported — and he called Stonewall Jackson with his army in the Shenandoah Valley to come to the defense of Richmond.

On June 28, 1862, Lee launched his attack against McClellan, bringing on a series of related actions that became known as the Battle of the Seven Days. Through tardiness on Jackson's part in putting his troops into action the first day, the Confederates suffered terribly at Mechanicsville. Lee kept his head, marched Jackson's forces through the night to where he wanted them, and next day battered the Union Army at Gaines' Mill.

Lee believed that he had licked McClellan and could easily crush or capture his entire army, but McClellan was shrewder than Lee suspected. This Union general loved every man in his army as though he were a son, and to save his army McClellan rose to heights of defensive greatness. Now he did what Lee had not considered possible — he moved his army across the Peninsula to where it could be under the protection of Federal gunboats on the James River.

So, as so often occurs in war, success and failure had followed in rapid succession. Lee had saved Richmond but McClellan had slipped through his fingers. The end was not in sight.

Fight for the Rivers

Meanwhile, there was a great deal of war elsewhere in America. Pioneers had moved along rivers to build a country, and now soldiers fought over those same rivers to control the country.

Increasingly a new name was in the headlines — the name of a squint-eyed stump of a general known as Ulysses S. Grant. Schooled at West Point, where he had stood last in his class, Grant appeared out of nowhere to win decisive victories, first capturing Fort Henry on the Tennessee River and then winning Fort Donelson on the Cumberland.

April of 1862 brought more disheartening news to the Confederacy from the Tennessee River. At Shiloh, in a surprise attack, the Confederates had seemed on the point of crushing Grant, but like Lee, he also had kept his head and turned disaster into victory.

Other disheartening news awaited the South that April. In Missouri, 17,000 Union troops under General John Pope cast covetous eyes upon Island No. 10, below Columbus, Kentucky. This island, which the Confederates had fortified, was the key to controlling the upper Mississippi River, and Pope wanted it badly.

An old wooden gunboat called the *Carondelet* — "She looks," said her skipper, "like a farmer's wagon" — was, however, the Union's actual hero in the battle for Island No. 10. The moon was lost behind an approaching thunderstorm when, on the night of April 10, the old *Carondelet* swept down the river with chain cable wrapped around her pilothouse for armor. On Island No. 10, bugles summoned the Rebs to battle-stations in the fort.

On came the *Carondelet* through the rains that now pounded down. The guns of the creaking gunboat flashed in the darkness. But the Rebs only saw her briefly — where her own guns barked death or when lightning streaked the sky. Overhead, the thunder rolled.

It was a fearful scene, really — the guns of the *Carondelet* pounding the fort, lightning, the thunder. And when it was over, Island No. 10, with 7,000 Confederate prisoners of war, was surrendered to General Pope.

Maryland, My Maryland

Since men rather than boats receive official credit for winning land battles, General Pope, as the hero of Island No. 10, was brought east to command the Union forces defending Washington. A man of strange moods and too many words, Pope bragged of the victory he would win. He issued orders that were senselessly harsh upon civilian Virginians, and whereas he may not have won many friends, he at least succeeded in making one bitter, unremitting enemy.

That foe was Robert E. Lee, who loved Virginia and Virginians more

than life itself. Lee was certain that McClellan, though still on the Peninsula, had no intention of again attacking Richmond. Boldly, Lee decided to move southward and handle once and for all the high-handed, loud-talking Pope.

In a series of brilliant moves, Lee so confused Pope that the poor fellow at one point was actually marching and counter-marching his army in an aimless circle. Finally, on August 30, 1862, Lee caught Pope in battle at Manassas Junction (called the Battle of Second Manassas or Second Bull Run) and so thoroughly thrashed his hated adversary that Pope soon was heading back west to live in relative obscurity for the remainder of the war.

Again, Washington quaked for its safety, expecting momentarily to see the Rebel army storming at its gates. But Lee had a bolder plan. He would carry the war entirely away from the soil of his beloved Virginia.

After all, there was strong pro-Southern sympathy in Maryland — or so Lee believed, at any rate — so why wouldn't many Marylanders welcome his army as liberators? He would divide his army, sending one wing under the ever reliable Stonewall Jackson to capture Federal troops and supplies at Harpers Ferry, Virginia. Meanwhile, Lee hoped to strike across Maryland into Pennsylvania, where by seizing the railroad bridge over the Susquehanna River at Harrisburg, he could cut off communications between the North and the West except by the slow, round-about route over the Great Lakes.

With his bands playing "Maryland, My Maryland," Lee marched his army across the Potomac. Then Lee, who was filled with surprises for the North, began to experience a few surprises himself. First, the Marylanders who watched his moving columns were far more hostile than friendly. Next, a strange accident occurred and a copy of Lee's secret order, revealing his full plan, was found wrapped around some cigars by a Union sergeant. McClellan, back in command, danced with joy at learning Lee was separated from Jackson. He'd get Lee this time, McClellan boasted jubilantly.

The Blues crossed Burnside Bridge in the Battle of Antietam.

Unexpectedly, McClellan struck Lee in a savage battle at South Mountain that ended at nightfall. For all the advantage McClellan had in surprising Lee, the best he could claim for that engagement was a draw.

Lee pulled his army back to Sharpsburg, crossing the stone bridge over the Antietam River and forming in line of battle between the town and the stream. McClellan, ever the hesitant, delayed a day and threw away his advantage, for now Jackson, flushed with a smashing victory at Harpers Ferry, came storming over the hills to reinforce Lee.

Next day, September 17, 1862, the armies clashed in "the bloodiest day of the war." In the damp, chilly dawn, the Battle of Antietam began along a sunken road that the soldiers renamed the "Bloody Lane." Around a little white Dunkard Church, across the stone bridge, through a cornfield, the battle swept in blazing fury.

The air, said a Union Army surgeon, was "vocal with the whistle of bullets and scream of shells." The cornfield, said a Confederate general, "looked as if it had been struck down by a storm of bloody hail." McClellan had reserves that he never employed that might have turned the day into a disaster for Lee, and nobody knows for sure why they were not used. Nightfall mercifully closed the carnage of this fearful day when each side counted its casualties at about 10,000.

On the following day, like a general stunned into numbness, McClellan made no move to renew the contest. A day later, Lee started for home, murmuring as his troops recrossed the Potomac: "Thank God!" He knew how lucky he had been.

The Year of Jubilo!

Since after Antietam the Southern forces had retreated into Virginia, Lincoln decided to regard the engagement as a "victory." The President was seeking an excuse to take a bold action that changed the entire purpose of the war.

Lincoln had been considering this course since June, when on many days he would arrive at the telegraph office in the War Department and sit quietly at a desk. Before him was a pile of paper on which, occasionally, he would write a few words, but for longer periods of time he would simply gaze out the window, lost in thought. A colony of spiders that lived in webs on the outer window fascinated the President and he came to know all their habits. Often, he stopped to read the latest war dispatches — not always the most cheering news. At the end of each visit, he carefully locked the desk so that no one could read what he was writing.

The pile of paper grew in the desk, and then one day in mid-July, riding in a carriage with the Secretaries of Navy and State, Lincoln revealed his mystery. Should the South persist in carrying on the war, the President said, he had decided to free the slaves as a matter of military necessity. Later, at a Cabinet meeting, the Secretary of State warned Lincoln not to issue his proclamation without a military success to support it or else the people would look upon his proclamation as "the last measure of an exhausted government." Lincoln couldn't deny that the secretary's argument made sense, so once more the papers were locked in a desk.

Now the Battle of Antietam — with Lee on the run — gave Lincoln the opportunity he wanted and five days later he issued his first, or preliminary, Emancipation Proclamation in which he warned that if the regions then in rebellion did not return to the Union by January 1, 1863, he would issue a second proclamation declaring slaves in those regions to be "forever free."

The South reacted violently. Some angry Southerners went so far as to cry that the time had come at last for the Confederacy to raise the black flag of piracy and offer the North no quarter! In the North, however, many were overjoyed by Lincoln's Proclamation, and in one of the great songs of the war they expressed their pleasure:

"Say, darkeys, hab you see de massa,
  Wid de muffstash on he face,
Go long de road some time dis mornin',
  Like he gwine to leabe de place?
He see de smoke way up de ribber
  Whar de Linkum gunboats lay;
He took he' hat and leff berry sudden
  And I spose he's runned away.
    De massa run, ha, ha!
    De darkey stay, ho, ho!
It mus' be now de kingdom comin'
  An' de year ob jubilo!"

Lincoln writing his Emancipation Proclamation in which he declared free all slaves in all states, including the ones still in rebellion against the Union.

With sound logic Southerners argued that the Emancipation Proclamation, by itself, couldn't free a single slave. Again, as in the early days of the blockade, the South taunted the President. Whom did he think he was bluffing? But once again Lincoln wasn't bluffing. He was reaching out — touching the hearts of people around the world — lifting the war above a legal argument to a ground where it became a crusade for human freedom. His Proclamation, wrote workingmen in England who had suffered from the loss of Southern cotton, was a "triumph of justice, humanity, and freedom," and they would stand by him no matter what sacrifices they had to make!

Single-handedly, really, Lincoln had won the first true victory of the war. He was saying in legal language what Northerners sang in their churches in "The Battle Hymn of the Republic":

    "As He died to make men holy, let us
        die to make men free,
    While God is marching on!"

77

Lee, the Invincible

Not by any means had Antietam knocked the fight out of Robert E. Lee. Rather, it was the Federal commander who seemed to be inventing endless excuses for not pursuing Lee, and Lincoln decided at last that he had suffered enough of McClellan's "slows." So the Union's powerful, big Army of the Potomac was placed under the command of another general — Ambrose E. Burnside, who wore copious side whiskers and rode smartly on a bobtailed horse, but who frankly admitted that he did not believe he was qualified to command an army.

And Burnside was right. Over hills that George Washington had roamed as a boy, Lee's army and Burnside's collided in mid-December, 1862, in the Battle of Fredericksburg. The core of that battle was a hill that the Yankees had to approach across a sunken road. Atop Marye's Heights, protected by a stone wall, were Confederate guns ready to belch death at any assault.

Six times, Burnside ordered his loyal troops up Marye's Heights. Six times, the Union boys charged and six times, the Rebel guns rained down a storm of lead upon them.

It was a ghastly sight, truly — the dead of one charge piling upon the dead of the charge that had gone before. Wave upon wave, the brave

Federal troops were defeated by Confederate forces under Robert E. Lee and Stonewall Jackson at Chancellorsville.

Bluecoats tried to storm Marye's Heights, and each time the Confederate guns were like scythes cutting down rows of wheat.

Once a single Yankee came within a hundred yards of the wall that shielded the Rebel artillery. There, for a moment, his comrades saw him — an heroic, defiant figure, waving his arm. Then he, too, was dead — just another sacrifice on that dreadful day.

Lee said at Fredericksburg: "It is well that war is so terrible — or we should grow too fond of it!" Staggered, the North read the reports from Fredericksburg. The Union's casualties had numbered 12,653, those of the Confederacy, 5,309!

When the third spring of the war arrived, the Army of the Potomac had a new commander in General Joseph A. Hooker. In Lincoln's eyes, he possessed one virtue that outweighed any shortcoming — he was willing to fight. In April, with the Virginia dogwood in bloom, "Fighting Joe," as he was called by his troops, moved suddenly above Fredericksburg, boasting that Lee and his soldiers had better pack their haversacks and make for Richmond.

Lee let Hooker march into Chancellorsville on the edge of that desolate region of Virginia known as the Wilderness. In this tangle of stunted oaks, where only owls, whippoorwills, and water moccasins could long survive, Lee met Stonewall Jackson on May 1, 1863. Together, they planned an unpleasant surprise for Hooker. While Lee held the front with only a relatively small force, Jackson would march the remainder of the army by a little known road around Hooker's right wing and crush the unsuspecting Federal troops before they could realize what had happened.

The plan, as brilliant as any the war produced, worked perfectly. Jackson crashed down on Northern troops with their arms stacked, preparing supper, and in the dusky twilight shattered them. Raw, nasty fighting still remained at Chancellorsville, but the Union forces never recovered their balance after Jackson struck.

Yet even as another great victory loomed, Lee lived through the days that followed in agony, for Jackson had been shot by accident by his own men. Stonewall's arm was amputated, and for a time he seemed to recover, but then pneumonia developed.

"God will not take him from us, now that we need him so much," Lee prayed.

But "Old Jack" had fought his last battle. His death plunged the South into tearful mourning.

Jackson was accidentally shot by one of his own men.

Hooker's losses at Chancellorsville were 16,845 against 13,156 for Lee. Receiving this news, Lincoln paced the floor of the White House, moaning: "My God! My God! What will the country say?"

Was there no general in the North who could win against Robert E. Lee?

Indeed, there was — just one.

Grant and Vicksburg

"He's hopelessly stuck in the mud," critics said that spring of General Ulysses S. Grant.

Grant did seem bogged down since he had brought his army from Memphis and camped on the high ground above the city of Vicksburg. This city, set on high bluffs above the Mississippi, was ringed with formidable batteries, for the Confederates knew that if they lost Vicksburg, they would lose control of the most important river in America.

To add to Grant's troubles, high water in the tributaries of the Mississippi that spring had covered wagon roads to a depth of 17 feet. But Grant tipped back on a camp stool, puffing on a cigar and thinking hard. The only way to win a war, Grant decided, was to do the unexpected.

And that was precisely what Grant did. If fortifications made Vicksburg impregnable to a frontal assault, then he would have to come at it by the "back door." So, loading his army on transports, he took it down river under the blazing guns on the bluffs of Vicksburg.

Grant knew that the Rebel army under General John C. Pemberton within Vicksburg waited to be reinforced by another army under Joseph E. Johnston — a juncture that he must prevent. Grant knew also that the rules of war declared an army must operate from an established base of supplies, but Grant decided to write his own rule-book. He would live off the land as he fought, cutting his way between the armies of Generals Pemberton and Johnston.

Quite before the Confederates had guessed what was happening, Grant had captured Mississippi's state capital of Jackson, wedged his army between Pemberton and Johnston, beaten back Pemberton's army in a fierce battle at Champion's Hill, and followed Pemberton to the "back door" of Vicksburg.

During the siege of Vicksburg by General Grant's Union forces, most of the townsfolk lived in caves dug out of hillsides. (See illustration on the opposite page.)

Here, however, he was stopped cold in two terrific assaults in late May. Again, Grant tipped back on his camp stool, thinking. If you couldn't win with bullets, then you had to win with bellies. He would besiege Vicksburg and starve out its defenders.

For six weeks, shells from Grant's cannon and gunboats pounded Vicksburg — as many as 150,000 on a single day, some said. Homes, churches, schools, stores, factories were smashed into rubble. Soldiers, old men, women, and children dug caves in the hillsides as Vicksburg was renamed the "Prairie Dog's Village."

A baby, born 12 feet underground during the siege, lived to tell the tale. Every day became like Sunday to those living in the caves. Food became so scarce that people even sipped a broth made of tree buds simmered in water. When the shelling stopped, folk piled up heaps of iron fragments, just for something to do.

Yet, stubbornly believing that Johnston and his army were coming to their help, the people hung on. Surrender? Never! In time they even grew accustomed to the shelling, and when Grant's guns renewed their fury, they grinned as soldiers ordered:

"Rats, to your holes!"

Gettysburg

In Richmond, Jefferson Davis faced the truth. Unless relief could be sent to Pemberton, sooner or later Vicksburg must fall. General Lee was summoned to an emergency meeting of the Confederate Cabinet. Should troops from the Army of Northern Virginia be sent to Vicksburg? Lee, always first a Virginian, shook his head. He spoke feelingly of what two years of war had meant to his proud old state — farms stripped of food, houses falling apart. His army needed everything — shoes, food, horses. Where could he find them? Lee mentioned the magic word: "Pennsylvania!"

So Lee again invaded the North. "It's like a hole full of blubber to a Greenlander," cried one of Lee's generals on beholding the rich farm lands of the Keystone State. Unhappily for Lee, his cavalry under Jeb Stuart became so entranced in chasing toward Washington to capture a Federal supply train that contact was lost with the main army. Lee had lost his "eyes" — the job of the cavalry, in such situations, is to spy out and report the position of the enemy — and Lee could not know that hard on his heels came the Army of the Potomac under still another commander. He was General George Gordon Meade, Pennsylvania-born and resolutely determined to defend the soil of his native state.

Unexpectedly, on July 1, 1863, the two armies collided near the sleepy village of Gettysburg. Lee's boys fought magnificently, rolled over Union troops caught in a railroad cut, and sent them flying on their heels through the town. A vigorous pursuit might easily have turned the day into a rout, but the Rebs stopped instead to celebrate their victory. Union troops that night occupied a height known as Cemetery Ridge.

Next morning, seeing the Yankees dug in on those slopes, General James Longstreet advised Lee to get out of Gettysburg. This was Fredericksburg in reverse, Longstreet insisted, with the Union holding the upper hand. But flushed with yesterday's success, Lee wanted to stay and fight. Scorching battles fought in sultry heat under overcast skies that day wrote strange names into American history — Little Round Top, Big Round Top, Devil's Den, the Peach Orchard, the Wheatfield — and here Billy Yank died beside Johnny Reb when night closed upon a contest still undecided.

Lee did not lose heart. On July 3, his cannon opened a terrific bombardment that stunned the Yankees on Cemetery Ridge. Then, across 1,400 yards of open ground, he sent the boys in Pickett's Division to storm the Union forces in their entrenchments.

Row on row the Rebs came, steady, brave, willing to risk anything Lee asked — then the Yankee guns spit flames of fire, and the rows of grayclad soldiers seemed to melt away. Others came up to take their places. Again the guns flashed, again the Rebs dropped, until all at once the utter hopelessness of Pickett's Charge swept over them and they turned and ran for dear life.

A courageous man waited as the Rebs reeled back across the field. "Don't be discouraged," General Lee called gently. "It was my fault this time." A faint smile touched his lips and he said: "All good men must hold together now." That night, Lee began his weary retreat to Virginia. Three days at Gettysburg had cost him 3,903 dead, 18,735 wounded, 5,425 missing. The Union's loss was 3,155 dead, 14,529 wounded, 5,365 missing.

A staggering blow for the South was Gettysburg. And next day — July 4, 1863 — brought an even more shattering blow when Vicksburg and Pemberton's army surrendered to Grant.

Union soldiers captured the fortified stronghold in the Battle of Lookout Mountain near Chattanooga.

Mid-Country

In September before Chattanooga, Tennessee, a Confederate Army under Braxton Bragg beat back a Federal Army under William Rosecrans in the Battle of Chickamauga. To this trouble spot rushed Grant. Finding the Union soldiers facing starvation or surrender, he forced open a supply route — his famous "cracker line." Then in November at Missionary Ridge in the "Battle above the Clouds," Grant's angry, snarling boys charged up steep hillsides, drove through ravines and over-ran Rebel riflepits until the Confederates, in Bragg's own words, were seized by "a panic which I never before witnessed."

Who now could deny one fact? In Grant, the North at long last possessed a *winning* general.

Grant vs. Lee

Congress revived the rank of lieutenant general, previously bestowed only upon George Washington and Winfield Scott, and in March, 1864, Lieutenant General Ulysses S. Grant was called to Washington to take command of all Union armies in the field. In round figures, Grant commanded 533,000 soldiers — a fighting force then without an equal in American history — and Grant's first move was to confer with his old friend, General William Tecumseh Sherman. They would divide the country, Grant said. While Sherman took the Western armies and smashed his way to Atlanta, Grant would "handle" Lee in the East.

In early May, Grant threw the great Army of the Potomac, which totalled 125,000 men at full strength, against Lee's Army of Northern Virginia, which did not number more than 60,000. The first battles were fought in the desolate Wilderness, where Hooker had met disaster. In this wolf's den, death came unseen among the oak thickets, for this was a contest fought more by ear than by eye. "It was not a war," a witness said. "Two wild animals were hunting each other. When they heard each other's steps they sprung and grappled."

But Grant was no Hooker, no Burnside, no McClellan. He knew how to use reserves — "feeding a fight," he called it — and Lincoln believed in him implicitly. Asked what was happening to Grant, the President replied cheerfully: "Well, I can't tell you much about it. You see, Grant has gone into the Wilderness, crawled in, drawn up the ladder, and pulled in the hole after him, and I guess we'll have to wait till he comes out before we know just what he's up to."

What, actually, was happening in the Wilderness proved a bitter lesson to Grant. Lee could fight — great guns, how Lee could fight! — and Grant was losing men two to one. But where other commanders of the Army of the Potomac always had pulled back when Lee had walloped them, Grant simply sought more favorable ground on which to continue the fight. Thus Grant began his famous "sidling to the left," a maneuver that pulled Lee after him until they were out of the Wilderness. Old soldiers in the Army of the Potomac cried happily, "Boys, we're on our way to Richmond!"

Lee's soldiers were devoted to him. "Well, boys," said a Rebel one

day, "the rest of us may have developed from monkeys, but I tell you none less than God could have made such a man as Marse Robert!" And how those hungry, war-weary, outnumbered Rebs fought for Lee — piling up the Union dead in heaps at Spotsylvania, following doggedly after Grant across the North Anna, the South Anna, the Pamunkey, then catching him at Cold Harbor and inflicting such dreadful losses that a shocked North began talking of "Grant, the Butcher"!

"I was wrong," Grant said after Cold Harbor. He was a big enough man, this Grant, to admit a mistake. If his "smash-'em-up" tactics wouldn't work against Lee, then he'd have to try something else. One thing was sure, he wouldn't retreat, for since boyhood, taking any step backward had made Grant feel dizzy!

So Grant began on June 15 to race Lee around Richmond to Petersburg. Here, both armies dug in within sight of each other for a stubborn siege that dragged through hot summer into a brisk fall, and then through a bleak and chilly winter into the spring of 1865.

Lee grew into a legend, and in Richmond there was talk about making him military dictator of the Confederacy. He was now the "Noble Lee," the old gray warrior who had been knighted in heaven and who, sharing the discomforts of army life, kept his sense of humor. Once when

Taking a lesson from Grant at Vicksburg, Sherman had the country feed his troops on his march clear across Georgia, making the South feel "the hard hand of war."

After the fall of Atlanta, Sherman and his soldiers burned the city to smoldering ruins.

he was calling on Mrs. Davis, and she brought him coffee in a fine China cup, he said good-naturedly: "My cups in camp are thicker, but this is thinner than the coffee."

Grant bogged down before Lee — the Confederacy took heart. But from the West came disastrous news. By a series of brilliant flanking maneuvers, Sherman had driven the Confederates out of Atlanta! Then from 3,000 miles away, and from Mobile Bay closer by, came word of Union naval victories that lifted Northern spirits and disconcerted McClellan, who that fall opposed Lincoln for re-election as President. The Democrats had placed their entire strategy on branding "Mr. Lincoln's War" a failure. But Sherman and Admiral John A. Winslow and Admiral David Farragut suddenly had cut the legs off that claim!

Gen. Sherman marched through Georgia to the sea.

The War Takes a Turn

Atlanta smoldered in ruins, burned by Sherman and his soldiers. "Where is Sherman?" a puzzled North began to ask, and even Grant admitted with a grin that his redheaded friend had disappeared like a mole under a lawn.

Sherman knew where he was going — clear across Georgia to the sea. Taking a lesson from Grant at Vicksburg, he would make the country feed him as he marched. The South had started this conflict, growled Sherman, and now it could feel "the hard hand of war." And Sherman said a great deal more that the South remembered bitterly — for example, how he would make "all Georgia howl."

You had to know Sherman's nervous temperament, and probe beneath his extravagant words, to realize that he was one of the shrewdest, best generals in America. As a boy, he had so hated his red hair that he had tried to dye it, but his hair had turned green, so he had learned to

live with it. Sherman was like that — hard-headed and practical, knowing that wars ended only when the resources for waging war were destroyed. And that was what he proposed to do — to go deep into the South, and destroy its capacity for making war.

In six weeks — tearing up railroads, burning any building that resembled a military installation (and a great many that did not), raiding plantations to feed his carefree, hungry "bummers" — Sherman cut a path of destruction across Georgia. Wheeler's cavalry and the local militia could offer only token resistance. Negroes shouted, "We's gwine whar you'se gwine, massa," and by the hundreds they followed Sherman's victorious columns. At night, the Negroes staged plantation dances and sang spirituals until after a time Sherman's boys insisted that the march to the sea was "just about as much fun as a fox hunt."

Comparing Sherman to a ground mole, Grant had added: "You can here and there trace his track, but you are not quite certain where he will come out till you see his head." Suddenly, Sherman's head appeared, and he had reached the sea at Savannah. At once, he sent Lincoln a telegram:

"I beg to present you as a Christmas gift, the city of Savannah, with one hundred and fifty heavy guns and plenty of ammunition, and also about twenty-five thousand bales of cotton."

"Many, many thanks for your Christmas gift," Lincoln replied, adding a confession: "When you were about to leave Atlanta for the Atlantic coast, I was anxious if not fearful; but feeling you were the better judge, and remembering that 'nothing risked nothing gained,' I did not interfere."

For Lincoln, the war was going swimmingly. But a big problem remained — how to end it.

The Confederacy's answer to the Union's naval blockade was to set loose upon the seas armed raiders to prey upon Northern merchant ships. The most successful of these was the *Alabama*, under command of Raphael Semmes, which during her career sent about 60 vessels to a watery grave and cost Yankee shipping a loss of approximately $6,500,000.

To find and to sink the *Alabama* became the dream of the United States Navy, and so shouts of joy arose from the Yankee crew of the *Kearsarge* when they sailed into Cherbourg on June 14, 1864, and found the *Alabama* at anchor in the French harbor. The *Kearsarge* waited off the breakwater for the *Alabama* to come out, and news of the impending battle brought eager spectators by excursion train from Paris.

They were not disappointed in the "show." On a bright, warm Sunday — June 19 — the lookout on the *Kearsarge* shouted: "She's coming out, and heading straight for us!"

When the two ships were 900 yards apart, Winslow, aboard the *Kearsarge*, ordered his first broadside. In a series of seven overlapping circles, the *Alabama* and the *Kearsarge* dueled. Winslow's boys, by far the better gunners, took their time — aiming deliberately, pounding home the shot from their 11-inch guns upon the *Alabama's* hull, piling the dead on her decks. Semmes knew his days as a raider had ended. Up went the white flag.

Then on August 5, 1864, a Federal fleet under Admiral David Farragut sailed into Mobile Bay. This old sea horse, who had been a midshipman in the United States Navy at the incredible age of nine, already had won fame by capturing New Orleans in 1862. As still an open port of the Confederacy, Mobile Bay was equally a prize and Farragut meant to have it.

At 5:45 next morning, when the fog lifted on a promising day, Farragut ordered his fleet into action. Disaster struck quickly when a torpedo plunged the lead ship to the bottom of the bay. Reputedly, Farragut shouted: "Damn the torpedoes — go ahead!" And putting his flagship in the lead, Farragut pounded his way past the blazing guns protecting the bay.

Now came the real fight as the Rebel iron ram *Tennessee* came out to smash Farragut's wooden ships. Straight for the Federal flagship, the

Admiral Farragut won a Naval victory at Mobile Bay.

Hartford, she headed. Union monitors swarmed around the *Tennessee* like snarling seadogs, and Farragut had himself lashed to the rigging to command the battle.

Eight-inch plates protected the *Tennessee*. Iron covers closed over her gun ports. But soon the *Tennessee* learned why Farragut was renowned. A Union shell knocked off the *Tennessee's* stack. Another jammed the cover over her port gun. A third smashed the leg of her admiral. Suddenly the *Tennessee* ran up the white flag. Farragut had knocked out the pride of the Rebel navy and Mobile Bay was won!

For Gideon Welles, Lincoln's Secretary of the Navy, it had been a fine summer indeed, and he felt at long last that he had avenged the poet who early in the war had written:

"Retire, O Gideon, to an onion farm,
Ply any trade that's innocent and slow,
Do anything, where you can do no harm.
Go anywhere you fancy — only go."

Now Welles could say that he had done more than his share — for the country and for Lincoln, standing for re-election. The impact of such triumphs as sinking the *Alabama* and capturing Mobile Bay — along with Sherman's occupation of Atlanta — surely would be felt when the voters went to the polls in November.

Many advisors had pleaded with Lincoln to cancel the election, in view of the national emergency, but he had shaken his head. The people must decide. They ran the government. Now on election night the President sat in the telegraph office of the War Department awaiting that decision. Early returns from Boston, Philadelphia, and Baltimore were encouraging. And then toward midnight, as more and more of the vote was counted, Lincoln knew — he would carry every state except Kentucky, Delaware, and New Jersey and win by an Electoral vote of 212 to 21!

With Malice Toward None

Actually, wars are not won on battlefields, but in the hearts and minds of men — sometimes in the heart and mind of one man, if he happens to be Abraham Lincoln.

One such victory Lincoln already had won when, through the Eman-

"With malice toward none; with charity for all . . ." Thus spoke Lincoln at his second inaugural address after his re-election.

cipation Proclamation, he had given a moral purpose to the war, and now on January 31, 1865, he won an even greater victory. Ten months earlier, the United States House of Representatives, voting on a 13th Amendment that would prohibit slavery throughout the nation, had failed to give the two-thirds vote necessary for passage. Lincoln, however, had interpreted his re-election as a mandate from the people to get on with the real work of the war, and had thrown his full influence behind bringing the 13th Amendment to another vote.

The signs all looked favorable. In recent weeks, slavery had been abolished in Arkansas, Louisiana, Maryland, and Missouri, and similar legislation was pending in Tennessee and Kentucky. So spectators crowded the galleries of the House when, at 4:00 o'clock, that last day of January, Speaker Colfax ordered another roll-call on the 13th Amendment. Anxiously, Senators left their own chambers and crowded around the door to the House. Name by name, the Congressmen voted. The tally clerk whispered the result to Colfax — Ayes 119, Nays 56. The amendment had passed by 63 votes!

Congressmen, leaping to their feet, danced in the aisles. The galleries burst into thunderous cheers and outside a battery boomed a hundred-gun salute. Lincoln could not disguise his pleasure. Passage of the amendment, in its way, he said, "winds the whole thing up." He congratulated everybody — himself, Congress, the country, the whole world.

"The Battle Hymn of the Republic" had not been meaningless after all: "As He died to make men holy, let us die to make men free." For the dead at Gettysburg and Vicksburg and 10,000 other places, there was a purpose.

Afterward, awaiting his second inaugural, Lincoln seemed to draw within his own thoughts, as though searching, searching, searching for the words to say one thing more that was in his heart and mind. On the morning of March 4, 1865, drizzle filled the gusts of wind from an overcast sky. Then Lincoln arose to speak — just as the sun burst through. And standing there in the golden light, he described the great triumph that the country had yet to win:

"With malice toward none; with charity for all; with firmness in the right, as God gives us to see the right, let us strive on to finish the work we are in; to bind up the nation's wounds; to care for him who shall have borne the battle, and for his widow, and his orphan — to do all which may achieve and cherish a just and lasting peace among ourselves, and with all nations."

The crowd watched as the tall man took the oath of office, then stooped and kissed the Bible. Old Abe — the man to whom they sang:
We are coming, Father Abraham,
Three hundred thousand strong . . ."

And come they had — and would still — and neither they, nor their children, nor their children's children would ever, ever forget how he had touched their lives and changed their common destiny.

To Appomattox

Only once during the entire war did the three men who shaped its final victory — Lincoln, Grant, and Sherman — meet face to face. The place was the steamer *River Queen*, anchored off City Point, Virginia. The date was March 27, 1865, and Sherman's "bummers" were marching northward through the Carolinas on their way to join Grant's forces at Petersburg. Lincoln hoped that the war could be ended without another costly battle, but neither Sherman nor Grant could give the President much hope on that score. Grant, leaving for Petersburg next morning, told an aide:

"I think we can send him some good news in a day or two."

Within a week Grant had smashed through at Petersburg, the Confederate government had fled southward, and Union troops had occupied Richmond. Lincoln visited the Confederate capital on April 4. "Thank God I have lived to see it," he said. Negroes by the hundreds ran to meet him, and Lincoln told them: "Learn the laws and obey them." Almost like a small boy, he sat in the chair which Jefferson Davis had used for so long in running the war against him. And to the Federal commander in Richmond he gave characteristic advice: "Let the people down easy."

Lee still believed that he had a chance of escaping from Grant on that April day when Lincoln visited Richmond. He drove hard for Amelia Court House, where he expected to find supplies for his hungry soldiers. They were not there. For five days, on courage alone, Lee carried on the struggle, but Grant's well-fed, buoyant troops were all around, pressing Lee into the little pocket of mountain countryside around Appomattox Court House and blocking the way on flank, front, and rear. Officers pleaded with Lee: "Fight on!" Sadly, Lee faced the truth:

"There is nothing left me to do but to go and see General Grant."

On Palm Sunday — April 9, 1865 — Lee rode into Appomattox to meet Grant not as a foe, but once more as a countryman. The two great generals of the war shook hands. Quietly, as gentlemen, they discussed terms of surrender that would be fair, under the circumstances. The documents were written out and Lee read them carefully, once borrowing a pencil to make a small insertion.

"I felt like anything rather than rejoicing at the downfall of a foe who had fought so long and valiantly," Grant said afterward.

At last, the papers were ready to sign. Again, the generals shook hands. Lee went out on the porch of the McLean House, where the meeting had occurred, and called for his horse. As Lee mounted, to ride off, Grant came onto the porch and raised his hat. Lee returned the salute.

Lee's army saw him coming back. The soldiers of the Lost Cause now rushed to the roadside, crowded around him, shook his hand.

"Uncle Robert!" some shouted.

"God help you, General," others cried.

Lee's throat tightened. He had to wait some moments before he could speak only these few words:

"Men, we have fought through this war together. I have done the best I could for you. My heart is too full to say more."

He turned then and strode to his tent — to be alone with his thoughts, his grief for the stricken South.

So the war was over. Some men shouted and danced. Some wept. Some wondered anxiously about the nation's future. One who faced that future bravely and wisely was Lincoln. On Good Friday, April 14, he spoke to his Cabinet:

"We can't undertake to run state governments in all these Southern states. Their people must do that — though I reckon at first some of them may do it badly."

With malice toward none, with charity toward all . . . Lincoln knew how the future of the country must unfold. But that night a dreadfully

On Palm Sunday, April 9, 1865, Lee met Grant at Appomattox — not as a foe, but once more as a countryman.

unbalanced man assassinated Mr. Lincoln, and at 7:22 the following morning the President died. Looking down on Lincoln's face, at peace in death, a voice at the bedside spoke softly:

"Now he belongs to the ages."

And the South had reason to grieve with the North, for it too had lost a friend — a great friend.

Brothers Again

The war had cost a staggering price. The Union counted its dead at 360,222, its wounded at 275,175. The South had 258,000 dead by a fair estimate. No one could guess how many Southerners had been wounded.

For what purpose? That, really, we knew deep in our hearts. In November, 1863, Lincoln had gone to Gettysburg to dedicate a National Cemetery. What the war must achieve he stated clearly:

". . . that this nation, under God, shall have a new birth of freedom — and that government of the people, by the people, and for the people, shall not perish from the earth."

Many of the problems that had plagued the country before the war still remained, but one did not. Slavery was gone and at long last the Negro in America had begun to be an American.

And we found something more — under all the anger, in the midst of all the fighting. We found ourselves. We came together, and the boy in blue who died beside the boy in gray in battle were really the same boy. In other wars, when the nation was threatened, they would stand side by side.

Poets know how to say these things best — and one who said it well was Frank Lebby Stanton:

"*After all,*
One country, brethren! We must rise or fall
With the Supreme Republic. We must be
The makers of her immortality —
  Her freedom, fame,
  Her glory or her shame:
Liegemen to God and fathers of the free!"

Stanton was born in South Carolina, the first state to secede from the Union.

97

Highlights of the War Between the States

1860

Dec. 22   South Carolina secedes from the Union.

1861

Feb. 4-8   South Carolina, Georgia, Alabama, Mississippi, Louisiana, and Florida form the Confederate States of America; Jefferson Davis becomes president and Alexander H. Stephens vice president.

March 4   Abraham Lincoln is inaugurated 16th President of the United States.

April 12   Confederates fire on Ft. Sumter.

April 15   President Lincoln calls for 75,000 Union volunteers.

April 18   Union forces evacuate Harpers Ferry.

April 19   Citizens of Baltimore attack 6th Massachusetts Infantry en route to Washington.

April 20   Gen. Robert E. Lee resigns from Union Army to join the Confederate cause.

June 17   Confederates are routed from Jefferson City and Boonville, Mo.

July 21   The first major engagement of the war is fought at Bull Run; the Union forces are routed.

July 22   Congress authorizes an army of 500,000 men.

Aug. 28-29   Union naval and military forces capture Fts. Clark and Hatteras in North Carolina.

1862

Feb. 6   Ft. Henry, on the Tennessee River, falls to Union forces.

Feb. 8   Roanoke Island captured.

Feb. 10   Elizabeth City, N. C., falls to the Union.

Feb. 16   Ft. Donelson, Tenn., is surrendered to Gen. Ulysses S. Grant, opening the way for an advance on Nashville.

March 3-4   Union forces take Amelia Island, off the Florida coast.

March 8   In the first battle of "ironclads," the Union's *Monitor* and the *Merrimac* (renamed the *Virginia*) fight an inconclusive sea engagement.

March 12   Union forces occupy Jacksonville, Fla.

March 14   New Berne, N. C., captured by the Union.

April 6-7   Battle of Shiloh. Confederates defeated after initial gains.

April 24-25   Union ships bombard New Orleans under Admiral David G. Farragut.

April 30   New Orleans falls and is occupied by Union troops.

May 3   Confederates evacuate Yorktown as Union forces press the Peninsular Campaign.

May 5   An indecisive action is fought at Williamsburg as the Confederates retire toward Richmond.

May 11   Confederates abandon Norfolk in the face of Union advance, scuttling the *Virginia* rather than leave her to the North.

May 16   Union Gen. George B. McClellan establishes a base at White House Landing, 20 mi. from Richmond.

May 31   Battle of Fair Oaks. Confederate Gen. Joseph E. Johnston wounded; command taken over by Gen. Lee, who withdraws his troops to Richmond.

June 26-July 2   Seven Days' Battle at Mechanicsville, Gaines' Mill, White Oak Swamp, and Malvern Hill ends Peninsular Campaign. Lee holds Richmond, and Union forces withdraw to the James River.

Aug. 9   Confederate forces under Gen. Stonewall Jackson defeat Union troops at Cedar Mt., beginning the Maryland Campaign.

Aug. 30   Gen. Jackson forces Union retreat in the Second Battle of Bull Run.

Sept. 4   Confederate army crosses the Potomac and invades Maryland.

Sept. 14   McClellan defeats Lee at South Mt., forcing the Confederates to fall back.

Sept. 15   Jackson takes Harpers Ferry and joins Lee before Antietam.

Sept. 17   In the Battle of Antietam, Lee's advance is halted, but he is permitted to withdraw back across the Potomac into Virginia.

Sept. 22   President Lincoln issues a preliminary Emancipation Proclamation warning that on Jan. 1, 1863, he would free all slaves in states still in rebellion on that date.

Dec. 13   General Ambrose E. Burnside, successor to McClellan, is defeated in the Battle of Fredericksburg.

Dec. 31-Jan. 8, 1863   Confederates are repulsed in the Battle of Murfreesboro on Stone River, Tenn.

1863

Jan. 1   President Lincoln issues the formal Emancipation Proclamation, thus freeing about 3,000,000 slaves.

May 2-4   Battle of Chancellorsville. Lee wins resounding victory despite the death of Gen. Jackson, who is succeeded by Gen. James E. B. Stuart. Lee begins invasion of North.

May 14   Grant takes Jackson, Miss., leaving Vicksburg open to siege.

July 1-3   In the Battle of Gettysburg, the decisive engagement of the war, Lee is driven back to the Potomac.

July 4   Vicksburg is surrendered after a six-week siege.

July 8   Port Hudson, down the Mississippi River from Vicksburg, is surrendered, giving the Union control of the entire river.

Sept. 9   Union troops take Chattanooga and drive Confederates back into Georgia.

Sept. 19-20   Confederates defeat Union forces in the Battle of Chickamauga, forcing them back to Chattanooga.

Nov. 19   Lincoln delivers the Gettysburg Address, in dedication of a cemetery.

Nov. 23-25   In the Battle of Chattanooga, the Confederates are driven out of Tennessee in two major engagements, the Battle Above the Clouds (Lookout Mt., Nov. 24), and at Missionary Ridge (Nov. 25).

1864

April 12   Confederates capture Fort Pillow, Tenn.; heavy losses are suffered by Northern Negro troops.

May 3   Grant, appointed Commander in Chief of all Northern armies, crosses the Rapidan to begin the Wilderness Campaign.

May 5   Gen. William T. Sherman and his Union forces leave Chattanooga on the Georgia Campaign.

May 5-6   Lee attacks Grant's forces in the Wilderness (a woodland area 10 mi. from Fredericksburg, Va.), but is unable to achieve victory.

May 8-19   In battles around Spotsylvania Courthouse, Grant continues to press Lee.

May 12   At the Bloody Angle, a Confederate stronghold, Union forces are repulsed after initial success.

May 14-15   Johnston tries to impede Sherman's progress but is pressed back to Resaca, Ga.

May 25   Union forces halted at New Hope Church, Ga.

June 3   Grant is unsuccessful in an

assault on Lee's forces at Cold Harbor, in the bloodiest struggle of the war.

June 14   The Confederate raider *Alabama* is sunk by the *Kearsarge* off Cherbourg, France.

June 15-18   Grant assaults and besieges Petersburg.

June 27   Sherman attacks Kennesaw Mt. but is repulsed by Confederates.

July 17   Sherman crosses the Chattahoochee River; Johnston is removed from command and replaced by Gen. John B. Hood.

July 20   Hood is defeated by Sherman's forces at Peachtree Creek.

July 22   The Battle of Atlanta results in victory for the Union forces.

July 28   Hood fails to stop Union forces at Ezra Church.

Sept. 19   Sheridan defeats Confederate forces at Winchester.

Sept. 22   Sheridan presses on and routs Confederates at Fisher's Hill.

Oct. 19   Confederates are driven from entire Shenandoah Valley by Sheridan's victory at Cedar Creek.

Nov. 16   Sherman heads southeast from Atlanta, ravaging the country on his way.

Dec. 15-16   Confederates defeated at Nashville.

Dec. 21   Savannah falls.

1865

Feb. 17   Heading north, Sherman takes Columbia, S. C.

Feb. 18   Union ships take Charleston, S. C.

March 2   Union forces win victory at Waynesboro, Va.

March 19   Sherman captures Goldsboro, S. C.

April 1   The Battle of Five Forks forces the Confederates to evacuate Petersburg, Va.

April 3   Richmond is surrendered.

April 9   Lee surrenders to Grant at Appomattox Courthouse.

April 14   President Abraham Lincoln is assassinated.

May 10   Jefferson Davis captured and imprisoned in Georgia.

Dec. 18   The 13th Amendment to the Constitution, prohibiting slavery within the United States, becomes effective.

THE
FIRST WORLD WAR

ENGLAND

KING GEORGE V

FRANCE

PRESIDENT RAYMOND POINCARE

RUSSIA

CZAR NICHOLAS II

Europe in 1914

The shot that triggered the War of 1914-1918 was fired by a 19-year-old student, Gavrilo Princip, in the little Balkan town of Sarajevo, capital of the Austro-Hungarian province of Bosnia, on June 28, 1914. Before its echoes died away, Europe was drenched in the most terrible blood bath the world had ever known; the war became known as "the First World War," because it was the first total war in history which involved whole nations, including civilians; it spread to 28 countries on six continents; battles raged on land from Africa to China, and on the seas from Jutland in the North Sea to the Falkland Islands in the South Atlantic Ocean; more than 10,000,000 men in uniform were dead, twice that many wounded, and more than 5,000,000 civilians killed; most of the European continent lay in ruins; the map of the world was changed; and "the war that was fought to end all wars" had set the stage for the Second World War 20 years later.

Bosnia had known a stormy past. Ruled by Croatian kings in the 10th century, occupied by Hungary in the beginning of the 13th century, it became an independent state during a short period of Serbian domination; conquered by the Turks in 1463, it became part of the Ottoman Empire. The scene of many insurrections against Turkish rule, especially during the beginning and middle of the 19th century, the powerful Austro-Hungarian Empire got a mandate after a bloody uprising in 1875 to occupy the country and keep the peace. In 1908, the Austro-Hungarian Government went beyond this mandate, annexed Bosnia formally, and made it a province of the Empire.

Many of the people of Bosnia, like Princip, were Serbian by ancestry and favored a union with other Slavic states free from Austro-Hungarian suppression, and now fought the Austro-Hungarian Government as they

GERMANY

ITALY

AUSTRIA-HUNGARY

EMPEROR WILLIAM II

KING VICTOR EMMANUEL III

EMPEROR FRANCIS JOSEPH

had fought the Turkish Government before. Many, like Princip, were members of the secret "Black Hand," a society of patriotic terrorists whose motto was "Union or Death." They thought they saw a chance for freedom when the Austrian Archduke Franz Ferdinand, heir to the throne of Austria-Hungary, came to Sarajevo on an inspection trip. A bombing attempt had failed in the morning, but as the car carrying the Archduke moved down the street later that day, Princip stepped out of the crowd, whipped out a revolver, and fired two shots. One struck the Archduke and the other his wife, killing them both almost instantly.

Princip's rash act was not, of course, the fundamental cause of the war. But it sparked the "dynamite" which had been piling up underneath Europe's placid surface for more than two generations.

Ever since the defeat of Napoleon a century before, England had been the richest and most powerful nation on earth. Her merchant marine and navy ruled the seas, and her army policed a colonial empire that girdled the globe. "The sun," Englishmen liked to boast, "never sets on the Union Jack." With raw materials from her colonies supplying her factories at home, England easily dominated world industry and trade. The pound sterling was the standard monetary unit in international finance. In virtually every aspect of world affairs, England was "top dog" — and she saw no good reason why things shouldn't stay that way.

On the continent of Europe, the leading nation was a young, vigorous, and upcoming Germany. She had won that position in 1871 after she had soundly whipped France in the Franco-Prussian War. Along with other spoils of that war, Germany had seized the province of Alsace and most of Lorraine, areas rich in mineral, farming, and industrial products. Soon, German products began to compete with those of England in most world markets.

To feed her booming factories, Germany needed more and more raw

On the opposite page, the heads of state of the Allied Powers ("Triple Entente"); on this page, the heads of state of the Central Powers ("Triple Alliance").

101

materials — and she soon acquired colonies in Africa and the Caroline, Marshall, Pelew, and Mariana Islands in the Pacific. This meant that she needed more merchant ships, and also warships to protect them. Kaiser Wilhelm II, Emperor of Germany, an arrogant, egotistical, ambitious young man, ordered his admirals to build a navy that was bigger than England's.

France itched for an opportunity to take revenge and to regain her position on the European continent. Britain peered fearfully over her shoulder at Germany's growing stature in world affairs. And so these two countries, France and England, adversaries since the days of William the Conqueror, suddenly found themselves in the unfamiliar position of allies with a common cause.

Meanwhile, the big Austro-Hungarian Empire was covetously eyeing the Balkan countries, and looking beyond them to the rich lands of the Near East. But Russia stood in their path. Russia, the largest country in the world, was also thinking about expansion — not especially in terms of more territory, but primarily to open up a passageway through the Straits of Bosporus and the Dardanelles into the Mediterranean for her merchant ships from the Black Sea. But the guns of Turkish forts blocked the way in these narrow waters. Even though its army, though huge, was the most primitive in Europe, and its navy a shambles, Russia, too, was spoiling for a fight.

In 1879, Germany and Austria-Hungary had signed a treaty which pledged each of these nations to come to the aid of the other in case of enemy attack. When, three years later, Italy joined the pact, this lineup became known as the Triple Alliance. By 1914, a similar mutual assistance agreement, the *Triple Entente*, existed between Great Britain, France, and Russia.

Thus the stage was set when the charge from Princip's pistol blew up the powder keg. The major European powers had already chosen their places on the stage.

Blaming the Archduke's assassination on Serbia, contending that Princip and his five fellow conspirators had received their guns and bombs in the Serbian capital of Belgrade with the knowledge and help of Serbian officials, Austria sent a stiff ultimatum to Serbia. It looked to a "police action," a localized war that would not only satisfy its urge for Balkan conquest but also serve as an opportunity to teach the Pan-Slavic movement a lesson and prevent other such anti-Austrian uprisings in other parts of the monarchy with predominant Slavic population. Germany encour-

The fall of 1914: The headlines of all the newspapers in the world, whatever the language, have one theme — news of the First World War.

aged Austria, being convinced that the powers of the *Triple Entente* would not interfere. Russia, fearing more Austro-Hungarian expansion and feeling compelled to do so as the major power of the Slavic nations, let it be known that it would stand on Serbia's side under any circumstances. Frantic diplomatic negotiations started, Germany and Austria still convinced that even if Russia would enter a war, France and England could be persuaded to stay out of it. None of the nations directly or indirectly involved, however, would risk the loss of face, would risk giving the impression of being too weak to fight or to live up to the commitments. Serbia would not bow to the Austro-Hungarian ultimatum.

Austria, refusing international arbitration, declared war on Serbia July 28, 1914. Russia ordered a general mobilization. So did Germany and France. In those days, mobilization meant war. On August 1, Germany declared war on Russia, and on August 3, on France. Great Britain declared war on Germany on August 4, after the German Army had invaded Belgium, whose neutrality had been guaranteed by England. The "localized war" Austria and Germany had hoped for had become within a few days a war between two powers of the Triple Alliance, the so-called Central Powers, Austria and Germany; and those of the *Triple Entente*, England, France, and Russia with the two small countries of Serbia and Belgium on their side.

(Italy, the third member of the Triple Alliance, deserted its allies, making the legal excuse that the obligation of mutual assistance existed only if one of the partners was attacked, but that under the circumstances, she didn't have to join her allies; they had declared war on the others.)

The Central Powers were joined on October 30, 1914, by Turkey and on October 5, 1915, by Bulgaria. The three powers of the *Triple Entente*, which became known as "the Allies" were joined by 22 nations, both great and small, before the war was over.

The War in the West to 1917

THE GERMAN ATTACK   A German plan for the quick conquest of France, the so-called Schlieffen Plan, had been worked out to the smallest detail by the head of the German General Staff, General von Schlieffen, 10 years before and then filed away in a top-secret drawer until the time was ripe. On the day Germany declared war, a huge German army of more than a million men moved swiftly to put it into action.

The plan called for four German Army units to pour through Belgium and thence down in a great scythe-like sweep through France. The primary objectives were twofold: (1) to capture Paris, and (2) to squeeze the life out of the French Army in the grip of a giant pincers. The fact that tiny Belgium was neutral — and that, moreover, its territorial integrity had been assured by Germany as well as by England and France many years before — made no difference to the German war lords. When this

treaty was brought to the attention of German Chancellor von Bethmann-Hollweg, he shrugged it off as being "just a scrap of paper."

The German General Staff calculated that they could polish off France before the bumbling Russian Army could even organize. Then, they would turn east and take care of the Russian Bear. The more confident estimates in Berlin were that the war would be finished in six weeks. Some of the more conservative generals suggested two months as more "realistic" timing.

German intelligence did not expect Belgium to resist. But the little

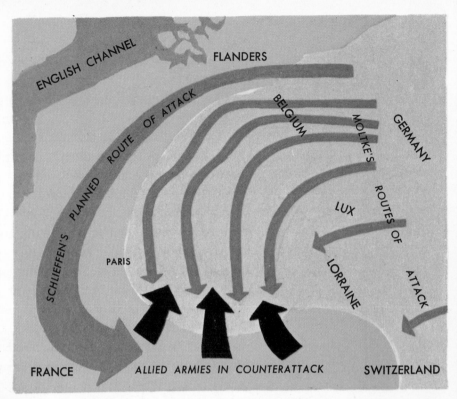

When the war broke out, General Helmuth von Moltke, who had taken over as Chief of Staff of the German Army, changed the stoutly designed Schlieffen Plan, which had envisioned an invasion through Holland and Belgium to avoid the French border fortresses. At the same time, a German army stationed in Lorraine was supposed to withdraw slowly in case the French would attack there and lure the French deeper into the trap between the big sweep of the main forces, with which the retreating army from Lorraine would finally unite for the last fatal blow. Moltke attacked only through Belgium and Luxembourg. When the French, instead of concentrating on defense, attacked the Germans in Alsace-Lorraine as predicted by Schlieffen, Moltke did not order a slow retreat of his army, but instead withdrew troops from the right wing, weakening it heavily, and tried to hold the French advance in Lorraine by launching a counter-offensive. While the Schlieffen Plan had called for a sweep around Paris, Moltke shortened the right wing east of Paris, allowing the French and British troops to make a stand at the Marne that finally stopped the German offensive.

The Belgium population trying to flee from the Germans often got in the way of their own soldiers, led by their gallant King Albert (inset above), disrupting orderly retreat.

105

Belgian Army, hastily put into the field by King Albert, fought courageously in defense of their homeland. In a matter of days, however, despite the help of French troops, their forts and their defensive trenches were pounded to a pulp by the heavy German siege guns. Brussels and Liege fell to the invaders. The population scattered throughout the countryside, trying to flee from the Germans; but they only succeeded in clogging all the roads, making any orderly retreat of their own soldiers impossible. They also got in the way of advancing units of the German Army.

In spite of the fact that King Albert's army was weak and badly equipped — some of their antiquated machine guns were pulled by the big shaggy dogs that normally pull milk carts through the streets of Belgian towns — their fierce fighting spirit held up the German advance long enough to throw the Kaiser's timetable out of kilter.

But even though it was slightly behind schedule, the grim German steamroller swept onward into France. The French tried valiantly to stop them, but they were no match for the Kaiser's men, who had been training for this campaign for 10 years. A small British force landed in France and quickly jumped into the scrap. But they, too, went down like ripe wheat before the relentless German scythe.

Despite the miscalculation that the Belgian Army would not fight, despite a communication breakdown caused by the destruction of French telegraph lines, the German Army stormed across two-thirds of France just one month after it had crossed the Belgian border, and reached the Marne River, only 15 miles from Paris. On its banks, French resistance stiffened. The French commander, General Joffre — his troops affectionately called him "Papa" — vowed the Germans would never go beyond this point.

Meanwhile, King Albert and what was left of his battered army fought their way into the northeast corner of Belgium, the famed Flanders, and dug in.

THE BATTLE OF THE MARNE .

In the lines along the Marne, 2,000,000 men were locked in deadly combat — a million on each side. The French and English were desperate. If they lost Paris and if they had to retreat toward the English Channel coast, they would soon be in the hands of the enemy. The Germans, on the other hand, were frustrated. The conquest of France was not going according to their well-laid plans.

At one point in the fighting, it looked as though the French line

would give way. Hurriedly, the French commander put in a call to Paris for more troops.

During the night, all of the taxicabs and buses in the city were rounded up to rush these 6,000 reinforcements to the Marne. Hundreds of vehicles streamed out from Paris. It is doubtful that "the Taxicab Army" turned the tide of battle. But it has come down in history as one of the great moments of World War I.

What really happened was that German General-in-Chief von Moltke panicked and changed the German master plan. In trying to pull the various parts of his far-flung "scythe" movement together, he actually opened up gaps between them which the combined French and British forces could attack piecemeal. When he lost contact with some of his commanders, a general German retreat was ordered in the confusion.

Von Moltke's army withdrew slowly from the Marne to a position nearly 50 miles from Paris. There, they dug into the ground and the chain of trenches that was to cut across Western Europe was begun.

The Kaiser recalled von Moltke to Berlin and fired him. The German grand plan for a quick and easy victory had gone up in the battle smoke along the Marne.

When the German armies were finally stopped at the Marne, the High Command devised a new plan. They proposed to strike northward to the English Channel ports of Calais, Dunkirk, and Boulogne, bring the southern coasts of England within range of their high-powered cannon, and cut off the British line of supplies.

In Belgium, British Tommies held the northern part of the Allied

BRITISH INFANTRYMAN

FRENCH
INFANTRYMAN
(THE RED
TROUSERS,
VISIBLE FOR
MILES, WERE
CHANGED LATER
FOR BLUE)

GERMAN
INFANTRYMAN

line as far as the town of Ypres. Beyond Ypres to Nieuwpoort on the North Sea, it was manned largely by what Belgian Army King Albert had salvaged after the fall of most of his country to the invaders. Fighting with the British were regiments of Sikhs, Ghurkas, and Rajputs from the British armies in India.

The Germans struck Nieuwpoort, Ypres, La Bassee, and Arras, the four main points of the Allied defense, almost simultaneously in late October. They were about to take Nieuwpoort when the Belgians opened the dykes of the canals and flooded the battlefield. With much of their artillery lost in the deluge and thousands of their men drowned, the Germans were forced to backtrack. At Ypres, they failed, too. They didn't have enough reserve forces to combat the combined strength of French, British, and reinforcements from Canada (who were, incidentally, seeing their first European action). Stiffened Allied resistance pushed them back, too, at both La Bassee and Arras.

The battle at Ypres was the last big battle on the Western Front in 1914. It raged furiously from October 20 to November 11, with one side gaining a bit of hard-won ground only to lose it to the other. But at last, the German attack was beaten back. Both armies settled down in their trenches, where they would remain deadlocked, for the next two years. When the fighting stopped for a blessed hour or two, communiques read: "All quiet on the Western Front."

In the first few months of the war, British cavalry vainly charged German artillery units. The toll they paid for their bravery was heavy (illustration on opposite page).

THE TRENCHES

Trench warfare was not new — but only once before in the history of war had two stalemated armies settled down opposite each other in permanent trenches for such a prolonged siege of nerves. That was at Petersburg, Virginia, in 1864 and '65, during the American War Between the States. But the trench warfare along the Western Front in World War I made the Petersburg campaign look like child's play. World War I veterans recall it as devastating horror, saying that the only way a man could survive it was to learn to "see things but not feel them."

By the winter of 1914, a system of opposing trenches snaked some 600 miles down through the middle of France from the English Channel to the Swiss border. They were hastily dug at first as emergency defensive measures. But as the weary months dragged on, they were elaborated into extremely complicated systems. Second-, third-, and fourth-line trenches

The battle at Ypres was one of the war's last trenchless battles.

were constructed behind the first line, so that the troops could retreat from one to the other in case of overwhelming attack. All of these lines were connected by communicating trenches. Supply trenches were dug from the front lines as much as three or four miles back, so that replacement troops and supplies could be brought up from the rear without exposure to enemy snipers.

Officers' headquarters and first aid stations were located in dugouts. Hot food was brought up from field kitchens in the rear areas. The soldiers who manned the trenches — some in their early teens, others with only three weeks' training — stood around miserably in the mud, fighting off the rats and vermin that swarmed all over them at night.

At all times, snipers manned the "firing step" from which they could look across to the enemy trench and pick off anything that moved. When a number of them were shot through the head, crude periscopes through which the men could scan No Man's Land without exposing themselves to enemy fire were devised.

At some places, the trenches were but a mile or two apart; at others, they were as close as 30 or 40 yards. It was this, the intervening yards of torn-up, shell-pocked ground, that was known as No Man's Land simply because no man could venture into it with much hope of coming back alive. On both sides, No Man's Land was bounded by the thick barricade of barbed wire that protected the front-line trenches.

Even so, patrols ventured out into No Man's Land nearly every night to try and find out what the enemy was up to. But before long, both sides began sending up flares which lit the night sky to high-noon brightness, and such patroling became even more risky. Actually, the patrols made very little sense, for both great armies were hopelessly bogged down.

At the crack of dawn, the heavy artillery from behind the lines began lobbing shells into the opposing trenches. And the bombardment usually kept up, off and on, all day. Soldiers just huddled deeper in their dugouts when the shelling started; hundreds of men were killed every day.

Every day or so, after the artillery bombardment at dawn, the men in the front lines would be ordered "Over the top!" in a charge that was meant to take the enemy trench by storm and capture it. But most of these charges, doomed to failure before they started, ran up against solid walls of machine gun bullets. On the rare occasions they succeeded, the trenches were usually quickly retrieved by men from the second and third lines of defense.

The longer the futile slaughter of trench warfare went on, the more impregnable the trench systems became. The commanders of both armies began to realize that the war was going to be a murderous stand-off unless one side thought of some sort of "secret weapon." Both the Germans and the Allies desperately set out to find one.

The Germans found theirs first. One morning in the spring of 1915, when the dreary warfare in the trenches had dragged itself out for more than six blood-soaked months, Allied soldiers at Ypres saw a yellowish-green mist move slowly toward them. It was chlorine gas! Behind the windswept clouds marched a line of German infantry.

The deadly gas finally reached the soldiers. Choking, blinded, vomiting, they ran in panic. Terrified of their own poison, the Germans advanced cautiously; now and then, vagrant puffs of wind would blow the gas back into their faces. The breaches made in the Allied line were but momentary; reserves quickly plugged up the gaps.

Gas masks were issued to all frontline personnel for protection from the gas attacks made off and on throughout the war. But horrible as it was, poison gas did not prove to be the breakthrough the Kaiser and his generals had hoped for.

Trench warfare on the Western Front went on and on. No one — on either side — could see an end to it.

SLAUGHTER AT VERDUN

It was the beginning of 1916 and the Western Front was still in the grip of a bloody deadlock. The glorious German dream of winning the war in six weeks had faded in the grisly reality of No Man's Land. Still, they held Belgium and all of the industrial areas of France. A dozen efficient railroads stretched back into Germany to provide an endless supply line. The German High Command now decided that the time had come for an all-out thrust in the West, one tremendous sledge-hammer blow that would end the war.

As their striking point, they chose the fortress city of Verdun, the pride of France. The battle that followed lasted for 10 months — from February to December, 1916 — and has gone down in history books as one of the bloodiest ever fought. In the slaughterhouse of Verdun, more than half a million Frenchmen were killed, wounded, or captured. The Germans had promised, "There won't be anything left living out there. . . ." Their casualties, however, were nearly as great.

The Germans opened the melee with a 12-hour artillery barrage during which more than a million shells pounded the French. On the

The tank, the British secret weapon during the battle at the Somme in 1916 (above left), was not too successful at first. By 1918, the tank, armed with cannons and machine guns (above right), was a formidable weapon. Our illustration shows 1918 models of French "land battleships" in action.

heels of the barrage came wave after wave of infantry. Yet, even in the face of this powerful steamroller, the French defenses held firm.

At the height of the battle, an unknown *poilu* (as the French privates were called) shouted: "Ils ne paseront pas!" And this "They shall not pass!" became the inspired French battle cry until the siege had at last ended.

The fighting raged with hardly a letup all through the spring, summer, and fall. It will never be known how many tens of millions of heavy artillery shells the Germans showered down on the enemy trenches, and the French big guns thundered back. The area between the opposing armies became a churned-up wasteland, spattered with shellholes, littered with the pieces of blown-up trees — and men. French soldiers said it was as if the enemy had pointed one cannon at each of them. Crazed by the horror, many men mutinied and others shot themselves. At one place, an entire trench was filled up by the debris of an explosion; only the tips of the soldiers' bayonets protruded above the ground. (After battle, the French left it as it was, a memorial to their brave dead.)

The Germans lobbed shells into the French trenches that were filled with a new and even deadlier kind of poison gas, so that the defenders had to wear gas masks around the clock. Gradually, the whole city was reduced to formless rubble.

Verdun was surrounded by a string of forts; some of these fell to the Germans after furious fighting. Later, they were recaptured in counterattacks just as fierce. About midway through the battle, some of the French leaders suggested that the army should fall back and surrender the city to the attackers. At this, French General Joffre declared that any officer who ordered a retreat would be court-martialed and shot.

Despite the power of their attack, despite their superior numbers, despite their excellent supply lines and the inadequate ones of the French, the Germans could make no headway against Verdun. By December 15, they abandoned their plan and withdrew.

If it can be said that any good came from the tragedy of Verdun, it was the fact that the heroic resistance of their men strengthened the resolve of the people of France to win — if only in the name of their dead.

THE BLOODY SOMME

While the fighting at Verdun was at its peak, the British mounted a massive attack against the German lines along the River Somme, a little more than a hundred miles to the north. Unfortunately, they elected to hit what was probably the Germans' strongest defenses on the entire Western Front.

General Sir Douglas Haig, the British commander, lined up 1,500 big guns along an 18-mile front, placing them about 20 yards apart. On July 1, 1916, this mighty battery opened up, spewing out a mass barrage of death and destruction, possibly the heaviest of the war. Thus began a bloody battle that raged back and forth for four months.

A look into the trenches, for so long "home" for so many — friend and foe alike.

"Over the top!" was the command that began the daily charges and that cost so many lives without changing a thing.

113

In July, 1917 — when what was officially called "the Third Battle of Ypres" and popularly referred to as "the Battle of Passchendaele Ridge" began — not much was left of the city of Ypres.

In many respects, the Somme was like Verdun. Although more than a million men died in the futile attacks and counterattacks, neither side accomplished anything of real importance. But each side bled the other white.

It was at the Somme that the British unveiled their "secret weapon." They intended it to be the key to the deadlock of trench warfare. And, indeed, it did much to change fighting tactics. The new weapon was the tank.

Brain child of British Col. Ernest D. Swinton, the tank was a heavily armored adaptation of the Holt Caterpillar farm tractor that had been developed in Peoria, Illinois. Manned by crews of eight, they carried either six-pound guns or machine guns, and rumbled along the terrain at a pace of four or five miles an hour. Officially, the machines were known as "land battleships." But for the sake of secrecy, the crates in which they were shipped to the front were labeled "Tank." This is the name that stuck.

When the tanks first made their appearance at the Somme, British soldiers were just as surprised as the Germans; and the Germans were terrified. The tank could move across trenches and crush machine-gun nests on its way, thus opening a hole for the infantry to attack through. The first clumsy tanks bogged down after a while in the battlefield mud. But new and improved versions were later developed by both the British and Americans.

The casualties at the Somme were even more ghastly than those of Verdun. The British lost 420,000; the French, 195,000; and the Germans, 650,000.

The British did not achieve the breakthrough that Haig had hoped for. They did, however, recapture about 200 miles of territory and push the German lines farther back. The Western Front settled back once again to the grim business of a war deadlocked in the trenches.

1917 — "THE FATEFUL YEAR"

The year 1917 began as a bad one for the Allies. The Germans were solidly entrenched behind what they called the Hindenburg Line, a defensive zone that was 20 miles wide in places.

At Easter, the British and Canadians attacked Arras where the Line's northwestern flank was anchored on Vimy Ridge. They made a little progress, but at a terrible cost in casualties.

All spring, the British had been digging a long tunnel under the Line at Messines Ridge. In May, they loaded it with a million pounds of dynamite and set it off. The ridge and the German trenches on top of it were blown skyward, and the British swarmed through. In the end, however, this advance was stopped, also.

In April the French, too, mounted a grand assault on the 50-mile German front from Soissons to Rheims. They were defeated so badly that the troops went on strike. General Nivelle, who had planned the ill-fated attack, was replaced by General Henri Petain, the hero of Verdun. He put down the mutiny and restored some semblance of *esprit de corps* to the discouraged troops.

At Passchendaele Ridge, in July, and again at Cambrai, in November, the British tried twice more to breach the formidable Hindenburg Line. Although Canadian troops succeeded in taking the Ridge and tanks, now perfected, were first used in mass (a formidable 324) at Cambrai, quick German counterattacks won back a large part of the Allies' gains.

The Eastern Front to 1917

At the beginning of the war, the Russians were full of fight. Their army, known as "the steam roller," and the largest the world had ever known, numbered 15,000,000 men. On paper, this looked like a force vast enough to mow down any opposition it came up against. But the figures gave a false picture.

Russia, country of illiterate peasant farmers, lacked the industry necessary to win a modern war. Consequently, they rushed to war deficient in artillery, airplanes, trucks, and motor cars. They didn't even have enough shells for the few big guns they possessed. The individual soldiers were armed, at best, with outmoded rifles. The Russian cavalry, the dreaded Cossacks, had a fearsome reputation. But as tactical military units, they were next to worthless. Moreover, the officers, selected usually for social reasons, were poorly trained; most of the non-coms, the corporals and sergeants who are the backbone of any infantry, could not even read or write. Radio communication and field telephones were all but unknown to the Russian forces.

Worst of all, Russia had virtually no railroads over which troops could be moved and supplied. Stacked up against the crack German armies, the dynamic German industrial complex, and the super-efficient

Sabers drawn, a unit of the dreaded Cossacks charges.

German transportation system, the stumbling Russian war machine was licked before it started. But the Russians didn't know it. Almost as soon as war was declared, the Czar's army moved on East Prussia, determined to take the fortress city of Königsberg, close to the German-Russian border on the Baltic Sea.

Southeast of Königsberg, they encountered a natural defense, the 50-mile-long Masurian Lakes. Accordingly, the Czar split up his army into two separate forces, one to attack north of the Lakes and the other to make a swing south of them. The southern army was commanded by General Alexei Samsonov; the northern, by General Pavel Rennenkampf.

Now, such was the sorry organization of the Russian armies that the two commanders had been bitter enemies since their youthful days. They did not speak to each other personally, and once they were in the field, they refused to communicate with each other.

The German commander in East Prussia, General Max von Prittwitz, with not many more than 195,000 men at his disposal, had received the difficult assignment from the German Chief of the General Staff von Moltke of defending East Prussia and halting the Russian armies until Germany was victorious in the West and could switch the armies from the Western Front to the East. He was torn between the desire to attack and the urge to retreat.

Rennenkampf crossed the German border with his 200,000 men or so on August 17, 1914. He succeeded in defeating the German troops in

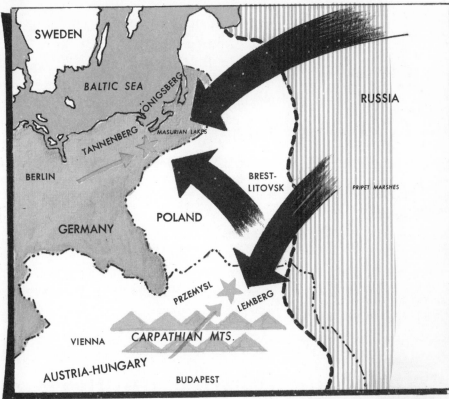

The map gives the locations of the major events on the Eastern Front.

his path and started his triumphant march on Königsberg. General von Prittwitz suggested to Berlin to order a retreat, even if it meant the sacrifice of East Prussia. Instead, the German Supreme Command recalled von Prittwitz and turned command of the armies in the East over to General Paul von Hindenburg, whom they had recalled from retirement, and made General Erich von Ludendorff, who had won praise during the Battle of Liége on the Western Front, his Chief of Staff. Together with Lieutenant Colonel Max von Hoffmann, one of von Prittwitz's staff officers, they made an excellent team which fully exploited the sorry situation within the Russian command. Von Hindenburg took over command on August 23 and was master of the situation just a few weeks later.

At Tannenberg, south of the Lakes, von Hindenburg pounced on Samsonov's army and — in the last week of August, 1914 — destroyed it. He then loaded his troops in railway cars, took them north of the Masurians, and gave the same bitter medicine to Rennenkampf one month later. In a matter of days, the Russian armies were reduced to a shambles. They

117

retreated pell-mell back into Mother Russia, and there they began to dig defensive trenches.

The Russians had better luck when they met the enemy along the Austrian border. In Galicia, their sheer numbers sent the Austrian armies reeling backward in defeat, and they penetrated deep into the Carpathian Mountains after taking the Austrian fortresses of Lemberg and Przemysl. The Austrian armies collapsed, but they were saved from utter disgrace by German reinforcements. Now the German Kaiser knew that the storied military might of the Austro-Hungarian Empire was going to be of no use to him. If Germany was to win the war, she would have to do it by herself.

The temporary Russian victories in Galicia were as devastating to the Russians as they were to the Austrians. The men ran out of food, guns, and ammunition. Pressed by the Germans, they slowly stumbled backward into that part of Russia which is now Poland. There, like their brothers up north, they dug trenches. And the war in the East settled down to the same frustrating stalemate as in the West.

Offstage in Africa and the Pacific

On August 23, 1914, only three weeks after the fighting started in Europe, Japan declared war against Germany. But the crafty Japanese had no intention of sending troops to help the Allies in France. The principal war aims of Emperor Yoshihito and his war lords were territorial booty and prestige. Japan's social and political sun had been rising since the Russo-Japanese War. Japan's true motives, however, would not reveal themselves until a quarter-century later; at the time, they were not considered.

Germany had established a colony at Kiaochow in the province of Shantung on the Chinese coast. Here, they had built a strong naval base for their Pacific fleet. Now, with the help of British naval squadrons, the Japanese attacked the German stronghold. After a three-month campaign, the German garrison surrendered. Thus, Japan gained its first beachhead on the Chinese mainland of China.

At the same time, Japanese and British fleets attacked and captured the German-held Pacific islands. As a result, the strategic Marshalls, Ladrones, Pelews, and Carolines were later mandated to Japan by the victorious Allies. And so, Japan got the South Pacific bases that were to

play such a vital part in her Pacific conquests of 1941-42 during the Second World War. By these swift moves, the Japanese adroitly took what they wanted out of the turmoil of the European war. Then, they settled back and watched the rest of it from the sidelines.

There were four German colonies in Africa — Togoland, the Cameroons, German East Africa, and German Southwest Africa. These were attacked at the war's beginning by French and English colonial troops. Sporadic fighting in the jungles and on the rivers and lakes went on for more than a year. The Germans could not spare troops from the European fronts for reinforcements. By the middle of 1916, German's African possessions were in Allied hands.

The bright German hopes of winning the war in a hurry were growing dimmer and dimmer.

Even though the fate of the German colonies was decided, one German officer still kept on fighting. Lieutenant Colonel (later General) Paul von Lettow-Vorbeck had been stationed in German East Africa when war broke out in 1914. For four years, he led the British a merry chase through its jungles. Even after German East Africa was cleared of regular German troops by the British, he and his band of guerillas remained uncaptured. They would appear out of the jungle, stage a sudden raid on a British outpost, and then vanish into the jungle again. He was the despair of the British, but in all that time they were never able to catch up with him.

On November 23, 1918, twelve days after Germany signed the Armistice, von Lettow-Vorbeck heard of it while leading his men on a raid through Northern Rhodesia. Still undefeated, he went in to a British headquarters and honorably surrendered.

The war comes to Africa: a burning native village in the Cameroons.

119

Turkey, Italy, and the Balkans

GALLIPOLI

Since Russia had practically no such industry of her own, she was dependent upon England and France for guns, munitions, and sundry supplies with which to fight the war. The Russians would repay their allies with shiploads of wheat and other foodstuffs. But the only route between the Mediterranean and Russia's Black Sea lay through two narrow channels, the Dardanelles and the Bosporus, farther north. Both were dominated by Turkey.

When, in November of 1914, Turkey, who had signed a secret agreement with Germany, came into the war on Germany's side, these two passageways were closed as tight as a corked bottle. For the Russians, this was disaster.

But young Winston Churchill, then First Lord of the British Admiralty, argued that the passages could be forced open by a direct frontal attack by battleships. He claimed that the operation would shorten the war by at least a year, perhaps two. Over the objections of some members of the British War Council, Churchill's plan, foolhardy as it was, was adopted.

In February of 1915, a British-French fleet of 16 major battleships, accompanied by mine sweepers and other auxiliary craft, steamed to the attack. In the narrow waters of the Dardanelles, they ran into a heavy field of mines, and a murderous cross fire from Turkish big guns in the forts along the shore. In the first attempt to force open the Strait, one French and two British battleships were sunk; the rest of the fleet, stopped cold, was compelled to withdraw from the hapless operation.

The British then decided to make a landing on the narrow Gallipoli peninsula, which lies between the Dardanelles and the Aegean Sea. Not only was this one of the worst-planned expeditions in military history, but the Turks knew all about it through information gathered by their spies in Egypt. They were waiting with big guns and barbed-wire entanglements when the first of the British forces began to land.

The result was a bloody slaughter. British and Anzac (Australian-New Zealand Army Corps) troops were mowed down by the tens of thousands as they tried to gain a toe hold on the beaches. Everything from the landing of supplies to care of the wounded was in a state of wild confusion. To make matters worse, there was no water on the Gallipoli desert, and men began to die of thirst. But for all the odds against them,

For the war in the Near East, both sides depended heavily on the so-called "ship of the desert," the camel.

The map shows where the major action of the war theater of the Near East took place.

the invading troops managed to secure a tenuous beachhead along the shore; there, they dug in.

The bitter, fruitless fighting went on for six months until the British leaders in London realized that the whole thing had been a ghastly mistake from the beginning and ordered a withdrawal. Winston Churchill, who had planned the operation, was removed from his Cabinet post in disgrace.

The campaign for the Dardanelles and Gallipoli was one of the most tragic of the entire war. Fortunately for Britain, Churchill profited by their lesson and survived disgrace to become one of "the Big Four" of World War II.

WAR IN THE NEAR EAST

In the fall of 1914, the British landed an expeditionary force of Indian soldiers in Mesopotamia, Turkish territory on the Persian Gulf, and quickly took the key city of Basra. Their objective was twofold: to protect British oil interests in that part of the Near East, and to weaken Turkey's war effort by encouraging the Arabs to revolt against their hated Turkish masters.

Sadly underestimating his foe, the British general ordered an advance into the desert to capture Baghdad, of *Arabian Nights* fame. On the way, the army took the miserable little desert town of Kut al Imara, which was nothing more than a forlorn group of mud houses baking under the scorching desert sun. Seeing no sign of hostile Turks, the British moved on toward Baghdad.

Within sight of the ancient city, the army was suddenly jumped by a Turkish force about twice its size. After losing nearly half his men in the battle that followed, British General Townshend beat a retreat back to Kut.

There, a huge Turkish-Arab army surrounded the trapped British troops and settled down for a prolonged siege. With scant food and water, almost no medical supplies, and no hope of relief, the Britishers were holed up in Kut for nearly five months. Men died like flies from hunger and tropical diseases. Finally, the pitiful remnants of the army, about 9,000 "dirty skeletons in rags," surrendered to Field Marshal von der Goltz, supreme commander for the Central Powers in Mesopotamia.

In the Syrian Desert, nearly a thousand miles west of ill-starred Kut, the British had better luck. After beating off an attack by Turkish troops on the Suez Canal, Lloyd George in London ordered the army to proceed into Palestine, which was part of the Turkish Empire, and capture Jerusalem.

At first, it was tough going. The Turks were used to the desert and the British were not; in the first months of the campaign, British defeats were severe. Then, a new general, Sir Edmund Allenby, nicknamed "the Bull" because he was huge and forceful, came out from England to take command. British fortunes began to look up. One of Allenby's greatest pieces of luck was his meeting with a strange young man named Thomas E. Lawrence.

Lawrence was a little fellow, scarcely five feet tall, but his body seemed made of steel wire. He had been an archaeologist digging up desert ruins when the war started, and had become the leader of the Arab revolt against the Turks after being sent to Egypt to head the military intelligence there. His men called him "Wrecker of Engines," because he had been harassing the Turks by wrecking their railway trains by blowing up bridges and tearing up tracks. He was to become famous in the history books as Lawrence of Arabia and for his own account of his adventures, *The Seven Pillars of Wisdom*.

Allenby decided to work with the little fighting rooster, and gave him almost limitless access to guns and supplies. It was the wisest decision of the entire Near East campaign.

Although he held the rank of captain in the British Army, Lawrence always dressed in the long, flowing native desert costume complete with sword and disdained all military formality. His Arabs were a wild lot, and only "El-Aurens" could control them. But they made the life of the Turkish Army miserable, surprising them in groups and often killing them to the last man.

Meanwhile, Allenby built up a large army. Just before Christmas of 1917, with Lawrence raiding the Turks and cutting their railroads and supply lines, Allenby was able to take Jerusalem. A few months later, again with Lawrence's help, he defeated the Turks at the decisive battle of Megiddo. This battle, in which Allenby captured 76,000 prisoners, was a decisive factor in finally eliminating Turkey from the war. Turkey surrendered on October 30, 1918.

ITALY, RUMANIA, AND BULGARIA

Italy was in the Triple Alliance with Germany and Austria-Hungary, but had refused to go to war against Britain and France in 1914 on the grounds that Germany was the aggressor. As a result, both camps tried to woo her to their side. Germany promised expanded territory; the Allies, part of Austria and colonial possessions in Africa. The Allied offer looked most lucrative; so Italy came into the war on the Allied side on May 23, 1915.

Italy was ill-prepared for war: Her army was far from up-to date. Her scant heavy industry would never supply a war

Specially trained and equipped Italian mountain troops prepare an attack in jagged Alpine territory.

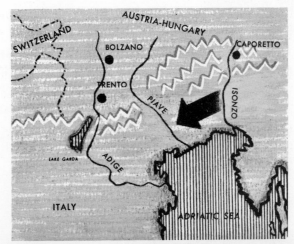

The map pinpoints highlights of the war in the Italian theater.

123

FOKKER D7

FOKKER TRIPLANE

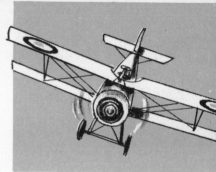

effort. Her people did not want to fight. When the Italians attacked Austria in the rugged Alpine country to the north, it had little effect. Nothing much was happening on the Italian front compared to the earth-shaking events in France. General Cadorna and his army had had to retreat when a strong German-Austrian army of about 400,000 men attacked the Italians in May, 1916, on the Isonzo River.

Then, on October 24, 1917, a huge army of Germans and Austrians suddenly struck at Caporetto, in northern Italy. The Italian line crumbled and the soldiers fled in panic behind the Piave River, where they made a stand with the help of the British and French. The disaster at Caporetto knocked the Italians out of the war as a national fighting force although Italian regiments continued to fight alongside the French and British on the Western Front.

Rumania, too, had been bargaining with both sides. Then, on August 27, 1916, she made up her mind to throw in with the Allies. Almost at once an Austrian-German army attacked the Rumanians; in three months, she was utterly defeated. Rumania's quick collapse provided Germany with much-needed oil from the rich Rumanian oil fields and thousands of tons of wheat from her rolling farmlands.

After having driven the Russians out of the Austrian lands which today comprise Poland, the German armies set out to finally punish Serbia. Belgrade, the Serbian capital, fell before the Germans and Austrians on October 9, 1915. Bulgaria, who hoped to recover territory lost in 1913 to Serbia, declared war on Serbia on October 11. The Serbian losses were terrible; and many Serbs fled to Albania and Greek islands.

Greece, torn between its King Constantine, who favored the Germans, and its pro-Allied Prime Minister Venizelos, for the other side, had tried to stay neutral but was finally forced into war on June 27, 1917, on the Allied side.

BREGUET 14
(FRENCH TWO-SEATER BOMBER)

DH-9A BOMBER (BRITISH-BUILT)

S.P.A.D. FIGHTER
(FRENCH-BUILT)

War in the Sky

The airplane was but in its infancy when World War I burst into flame in 1914. The Wright brothers had made their first faltering heavier-than-air flights — the longest of which had lasted less than a minute — only 11 years before. Yet, the airplane developed faster and further in the four years of the war than any other weapon in history in a comparable period of time.

In the beginning, flimsy biplanes, built like the original Wright pusher, flew over opposing lines to observe the movements of enemy troops. Sometimes, a British pilot would pass close to a German pilot. On these occasions, both fliers would wave a gallant salute to each other. High above the filthy mud and blood of the battlefield below, they felt that they were knights of the sky.

Then one day, one of these British "knights" got an idea. He put a pistol into the pocket of his flying suit. The next time a German plane flew within range, instead of saluting, he fired. After that, all the pilots on both sides carried hand guns, and the brief age of chivalry in the air was finished.

Within the next year, airplane design advanced tremendously. The Wright-type "Flier" gave way to a comparatively solidly-built ship with biplane wings and an engine mounted in front of the fuselage. A light machine gun, secured to the top wing, fired over the propeller. This was an awkward arrangement, however, for it was almost impossible for a pilot to aim his gun at an enemy plane.

Then, a young Dutchman named Anthony Fokker, who designed fighter planes for the Germans, began to ponder the problem. He later related that he got his great idea one night after he had gone to bed, jumped up, went to his drawing board, and had the whole design on paper by morning. The conception was simplicity itself — to an engineer. Let the motor fire the gun! And synchronize it, so that the bullets would pass through the propeller blades when the blades were out of the line of fire! Now, the German pilot could aim his plane directly at an enemy craft and knock it down with precision.

For several months, this revolutionary gun gave the Germans a decided advantage in aerial warfare. Allied pilots were calling themselves "Fokker fodder." But it didn't take British and French engineers long to catch on to what Fokker had done. When they did, German and Allied fliers were fairly evenly matched. Their planes, highly maneuverable, could fly from 100 to 140 miles per hour. Most of the victories then went to the pilots with the greatest flying skill.

Although by 1917, both sides had developed large bombing planes that carried one or two men besides the pilot, aerial bombardment did not play too decisive a part in the battles of World War I. Scouting and observation (reconnaissance) continued to be the prime function of the air forces.

A more glamorous use of the plane, however, in the war — and the one that made newspaper headlines — was the shooting down of enemy aircraft. Any pilot who destroyed five or more enemy planes was designated as an "ace."

The leading ace was a German, Baron Manfred von Richthofen, "the Red Knight," who had 80 single-handed kills to his credit before he in turn was shot down in flames by a kid from Canada named Roy Brown. Captain Rene Fonck was the top French ace with a score of 75. Captain Edward Mannock held the British record of 73. Close on his heels was Canadian Major Billy Bishop with his 72. (In World War II, Bishop was Air Marshal of the Royal Canadian Air Force.)

The American "Ace of Aces" was Captain Eddie Rickenbacker, a former automobile test driver who had started out in the war as General Pershing's chauffeur. He scored 26 victories during the few months that United States fighting planes were active. After the war, Captain Rickenbacker organized, and is now president of, one of America's leading commercial airlines.

One of the most terrifying aircrafts — to civilians, at least — developed during the war was the German Zeppelin. It had been invented several years before by a German scientist, Count Ferdinand Zeppelin, as a peacetime passenger-carrying airship. But the Kaiser's High Command at once saw its possibilities for the bombing of English cities, specifically London.

"The Zep," as it was called, was a lighter-than-air craft, shaped like a huge cigar and nearly 700 feet long, about the length of two and a half

In 1916, American volunteers in Europe formed the *Lafayette Escadrille* which went over to American Army command after the U.S.A. entered the war in 1917. The Indianhead emblem on the fuselage identifies the plane, piloted by an American flier, as one belonging to the famous *Lafayette Escadrille* (above).

Both sides used lighter-than-air craft in the form of observation balloons. In the German "sausage balloon," the observer, in a wicker basket hanging from the balloon, kept a close eye on the front (at right).

football fields. Through the middle, it was 72 feet thick. Its framework was a light but strong aluminum alloy covered with airplane cloth. It was buoyed up, like a balloon, by hydrogen gas. Six engines propelled it through the air at a top speed of about 60 miles per hour. It carried an observation car that could be lowered by a thousand feet of steel cable. Thus, the Zeppelin was able to sail along above the clouds while the observer swung beneath them and reported his findings by phone.

Crew quarters were inside the hull; crews on duty rode in twin gondolas slung underneath the ship. The Zeps were armed with machine guns and light cannons — and they carried 300 fire bombs!

But for all its formidable appearance, the Zep had a number of severe drawbacks. Hydrogen gas, for one thing, is highly inflammable. If the ship was hit by an incendiary bullet, or if any sort of stray spark was struck inside it, the entire craft exploded in a furious burst of flame. So, Zep crews really had the most dangerous jobs of the war. Moreover, being lighter than air and bulky, the Zep was almost impossible to control in a high wind.

ALBATROSS D3

FOKKER E4

The Germans hoped that their Zeppelin fleet, by burning the city of London and destroying English industry, might bring the English people to their knees. But, like poison gas, it was another "secret weapon" that failed. The Zeps did their bombing at night, and at first, the civilian population was terrified. But soon, they found that the German bombs did little real damage, and relatively few people were killed. After a number of raids, so many Zeps were shot down in flames that the Germans concluded that the results were not worth the cost. They called the bombing campaign off.

Actually, the Zeppelins had an effect the Germans never expected. The ruthless killing of innocent women and children and the demolishment of their homes infuriated the British people and stiffened their will to defeat the German "murderers." In the United States, people were horrified at such wanton brutality. America was brought a step closer to entering the war on the side of the Allies.

The Zeppelin, a hu[ge] lighter-than-air dirig[i]ble, did not fulfill t[he] expectations of t[he] German High Co[m]mand. Many explod[ed] and burned.

German U-boat on blockade duty stops a British supply ship. The Allied crew takes to the lifeboats.

The War at Sea

Next to Britain, Germany had the most powerful navy in the world. But the German fleet was based at Kiel, in a bay of the Baltic Sea, and it was almost impossible for the battleships and cruisers to put to sea without being detected and engaged by the British. For the first two years of the war, the German fleet practically rusted at its moorings in its home harbor.

Meanwhile, British warships were able to rove the world's oceans almost at will and clear the seas of German ships, both merchant and naval. Within a few months after the war began, the British Navy had clamped down an effective blockade.

Early in the fighting, then, it became apparent that Germany would have to rely on her submarines for action on the high seas. They called their undersea boats "U-Boats." German shipyards desperately worked to build a large U-Boat fleet as rapidly as they could. This was another of their tries at a "secret weapon."

In the spring of 1915, Germany boldly announced to the world that U-Boats would sink any Allied ships that appeared within certain specified "war zones" without warning. All ships, even those from neutral countries carrying supplies to England, were considered enemies. All of the neutrals, including the United States, protested what they considered "uncivilized" warfare. But the Germans replied that their U-Boats would continue to prowl the seas until the stranglehold on them was broken. It is estimated

After America entered the war, merchant ships and troop transports, protected by warships, traveled in convoys through the U-boat blockade.

Deadly torpedoes are loaded aboard a U-boat. One of them hit the British luxury liner "Lusitania" on May 7, 1915, and sank her in a matter of minutes. This was one of the events which brought America into the war on the side of the Allies.

that during the course of the War, more than 4,000 ships, neutral as well as Allied, were sent to the bottom by German subs. Like the Zeppelin raids, the unrestricted U-Boat campaign had an adverse effect for the Germans. Public opinion in the United States turned sharply against Germany.

The turning point in the U-Boat war came on May 7, 1915. A week before, the *Lusitania*, Britain's newest and fastest luxury liner, had sailed from New York for Liverpool. Aboard her were 197 Americans, including women and children. Only a few miles off the Irish coast, she was struck by a torpedo from a submerged U-Boat. The stricken *Lusitania* sank in a matter of minutes, taking some 1,200 of her passengers with her to the bottom. Among the dead were 115 of the 197 Americans. The Germans

First came destroyers; then, cruisers and torpedo boats (with observation balloons) followed by files of merchant ships, flanked by trawlers for protection against torpedoes. More torpedo boats formed a rear guard. Destroyers circled the convoy constantly to engage and sink enemy U-boats.

defended the sinking by claiming that the *Lusitania* had been carrying munitions.

The people of the United States were outraged; "Remember the *Lusitania*" became a rallying cry for war. It was only a question of time until the U. S. would enter the war on the side of the Allies.

There was only one major naval battle during the entire course of the war between the German High Seas Fleet and the British Grand Fleet. It took place on May 31, 1916, in the North Sea off the Danish peninsula of Jutland.

On May 30, Admiral Scheer, Commander in Chief of the German fleet, sailed into the North Sea with virtually all his heavy battleships, escorted by cruisers and destroyers. His purpose was to try to come to grips with the British Grand Fleet and destroy it. A fighting admiral, he saw no point in a huge navy that simply stayed in its harbor and saw no action.

What Admiral Scheer didn't know, however, was that the British had broken the secret German code and thus, were warned of his plans. The British Commander, Admiral Jellicoe, at once took the Grand Fleet to sea to hunt down the Germans.

The two fleets clashed the next day, May 31. The main action, obscured by great clouds of black powder smoke, lasted only about two hours. But by the time the furious fighting was over and the battle smoke had cleared away, the British had lost three battle cruisers, three armored

A German U-boat blows up her prize after the crew has abandoned ship.

The height of the Battle of Jutland: Scheer's battleships attack once again.

cruisers, and eight destroyers. The German losses were one battleship, one battle cruiser, four light cruisers, and five destroyers. The British loss in lives was 6,097; the German, 2,545.

The young man who was later to become King George VI of England when his elder brother, Edward VIII, abdicated, fought as a junior officer on one of the British battleships.

But for all its sound and smoke and fury, the great sea battle proved nothing. When it was over, the German High Seas Fleet went back to its base to remain there, doing nothing, for the rest of the war. And the British retained their old command of the seas.

Close-up of the deck and turrets of the German battle cruiser "Seydlitz," heavily damaged during the Battle of Jutland.

133

The Course of the War 1917-1918

THE RUSSIAN REVOLUTION

GRIGORI EFIMOVICH
ALIAS RASPUTIN

Revolution had been brewing in Russia for a great many years before the war began. The Russian peasants owned no land of their own and lived in misery and want. The factory workers were little better than slaves, barely managing to eke out a meagre living from long hours of toil. The ruling classes were rich and all-powerful, and had no understanding or sympathy for the plight of the laboring masses.

Yet when war was declared, the Russian people responded with patriotic fervor, and rushed to the colors by the millions. But the eagerness of the common soldiers soon turned to gloom. Some of the men actually had no rifles. Food was scarce. Thousands went without shoes in the freezing Russian winters, and had to wrap their feet with rags.

Moreover, Russian casualties at the front were appalling. In one campaign — a futile effort to push the Austrians and Germans out of Poland in 1915 — the Russians lost more than a million men. The Russian soldier was just about ready to quit. All that was needed was a spark to light the fire. Ironically, it was set off in the palace of the Czar.

Since birth, the Czar's small son had been a victim of hemophilia, a rare blood disease which can cause its victim to bleed to death from even the smallest cut. The royal doctors could do nothing for it.

In 1905, a lay monk had appeared in Moscow to become known as a "holy man," able to heal many ailments for which doctors knew no cure. His name was Grigori Efimovich, but he became known in history as Rasputin (really his nickname). He appeared a few years later in St. Petersburg as the leader of a new religious cult and was introduced at the court in 1907. He soon gained tremendous influence there in all matters, especially after the Czar and Czarina became convinced of his ability to cure their ailing son. When his political influence got in the way of some leading noblemen, the Czar was forced to banish him to Siberia in 1913, but he returned to St. Petersburg soon after the outbreak of the war to be received with renewed favour by the court. A sinister political influence, he coerced the Czar to hire and fire certain high officials, and his evil way of life lost for Czar Nicholas the little respect he had left.

Late in 1916, a group of noblemen succeeded in assassinating Rasputin, but the damage had been done by then. Revolutionary mobs stormed through all Russian cities crying for the end of the Czar's rule.

Ordered to fire on the crowds, the soldiers refused and joined the Revolutionaries. A few months later, in March, 1917, the Czar was forced to abdicate his throne, and he and his family were imprisoned and executed not long afterwards.

The leader of the Revolution, Kerensky, formed a new Socialist government intent on carrying on the war on the side of the Allies. The Russian soldiers, however, had had enough of fighting. When a new offensive was ordered on the Galician front by General Brusilov, the soldiers refused to move, formed councils and elected their own leaders, left the ranks of the army, and started to walk home to get their share in the land of the rich promised them. Kerensky's government was overthrown by Lenin, the Communist leader, whom the Germans had helped smuggle into the country from exile in Switzerland.

Unable and unwilling to carry on the war, Lenin's government negotiated and signed on March 3, 1918, the peace treaty of Brest-Litovsk. The terms were harsh. The Russians had to give up most of their territory in eastern Europe, which meant half a million square miles of fertile wheatland and industry and 56,000,000 people. Most advantageous at the moment for the Germans, this separate treaty allowed them to release their troops from the Eastern Front for use in the West. For Britain and France, it was the war's lowest point.

Lenin addresses a meeting during the Russian Revolution.

Soldiers, sailors, and workers storm the Winter Palace in Petrograd, once St. Petersburg, on November 7, 1917. The far-reaching Bolshevik Revolution under Lenin's leadership had begun.

135

UNCLE SAM DECLARES WAR

At the war's beginning, the people of the United States were determined to stay out of it, and to trade with both sides impartially. Most American sentiment was on the side of Britain and France, but there were also millions of Americans of German descent who sympathized with "the Fatherland." But on one thing, everybody agreed — it was Europe's private fight and none of our business.

Little by little, however, Americans began to turn sharply against Germany. People were appalled at the ruthless invasion of neutral Belgium, the inhuman use of poison gas, the Zeppelin raids on London, the sinking of unarmed ships by U-Boats. When the *Lusitania* was torpedoed and innocent American lives were lost, this indignation reached a crescendo.

And the Germans did many other things that antagonized the

February 2, 1917: President Wilson announcing to Congress the breaking-off of diplomatic relations with Germany prior to Congress' declaration of war on April 6, 1917.

American people. They sent spies into the United States to blow up munition factories as well as munition ships in the harbors. German agents, it was said, planned to poison drinking water in reservoirs in American cities.

Then, in February, 1917, the German Foreign Secretary, Alfred Zimmermann, made a very stupid move. He sent a note to the German ambassador in Mexico in which he proposed that if the United States entered the war against Germany, Mexico should immediately make war on the United States. Mexico's spoils of victory would be territory in Texas, New Mexico, and Arizona which had been lost to Mexico as a result of the Mexican War in 1848. The Zimmermann note was intercepted by the British and printed in American newspapers.

Ten days after this note was published, Germany announced a policy of completely unrestricted submarine warfare. Their U-Boats would sink any ship on sight regardless of the flag she flew, if the U-Boat commander had reason to believe that she was carrying goods to the Allies. This was the worst mistake the Germans could possibly have made. But by this time, they were so deeply involved that it was a case of "whole hog" or none at all. Besides, they were supremely confident of victory.

These two events, the Zimmermann note and the announcement of unrestricted submarine warfare — coming as they did only ten days apart — were the last straw. America made up her mind. On April 6, 1917, Congress declared war on Germany.

War fever ran high all over the country, but the United States was

George M. Cohan's rousing "Over There" became the theme song of America's fighting men.

The Yanks are coming. April, 1918: The first American troops disembark in French harbors. More than 100,000 men followed in the first month alone. Wherever they showed up, they were greeted by the French population with wild cheers and flowers.

The going was tough for the attacking American troops on the Meuse-Argonne front.

sadly unprepared to fight. Our Army was small and old-fashioned. Our Air Force was practically non-existent. Our Navy had been allowed to go to seed. America's first task was to build up an efficient fighting force.

"Preparedness" became a national crusade, and "The Yanks Are Coming" was heard all over the 48 states. Almost a million and a half men were selected in the first draft. Dozens of training camps were rapidly set up. General John J. ("Black Jack") Pershing, a seasoned veteran, was placed in supreme command.

With the Russian front collapsed, the French and British had their backs to the wall. They fervently prayed that the Americans would get to France in time.

And they did. A little more than a year later, early in the summer of 1918, a U.S. Army of 2,000,000 men, well-equipped and well-trained, landed in France and moved into the front lines. With their coming, the Germans were doomed.

THE YANKS GO INTO ACTION

In the spring of 1918, American troops, a division at a time, began arriving in France to go into training camps there. But it would be another two or three months before the A.E.F. (American Expeditionary Force) got to the front in large numbers. The French and British Armies were war-weary and discouraged by defeat. On the other hand, the Germans were being reinforced by troops released from the Russian front. Now, the German leaders thought, was the time for an all-out attack.

The German General Ludendorff began his attack on March 21 with a dramatic show of strength. For the first time, the Germans unveiled a giant cannon which they affectionately called "Big Bertha." Set up behind the Hindenburg Line, it could lob a shell into Paris, 75 miles away. At the top of its trajectory, the shell traveled 21 miles into the air. The world was flabbergasted at this stunning display of German science. The people of Paris were badly frightened. But for all her thunder, Big Bertha did very little real damage.

With the initial roar of the big gun, the German offensive struck. At the first fierce impact, it rolled back the British and French defenses. But after retreating foot by foot for 50 miles, the British line stiffened and held. The German advance was momentarily halted.

Then in May, Ludendorff moved forward again. This time, at the little village of Château-Thierry on the River Marne, the Germans ran into several A.E.F. Divisions that Pershing had rushed to the front. Like demons, the Yanks attacked and stopped them cold.

Not far from Château-Thierry was the German stronghold of Belleau Wood, a rough, forested area. A battalion of U.S. Marines was ordered to capture it. Advancing into the face of overpowering machine-gun fire, as well as clouds of poison gas, the brave Marines took the Wood. But they paid a terrible price for victory: more than half their number were killed or wounded.

The German advance was at last stopped, only 40 miles from Paris. And the Yanks had done it! German defeat was only a matter of time.

THE ALLIES ATTACK

The German Armies made one final desperate offensive drive in July. After a hard fight, American and French divisions, fighting shoulder to shoulder, turned them back at what is known as the Second Battle of the Marne. At long last, the German war machine—that had trampled so arrogantly across the Belgian border four years before—was on the defensive.

The stage was set for the Allied push that would end the war.

It would be a two-prong pincer attack, with a million Yanks under General Pershing pushing north through the Argonne Forest, east of Verdun; and an equally large army of British and French, under General Haig, breaking through in the Vimy-Arras sector. Other smaller Allied units, one of them led by Belgian King Albert, would strike the Hindenburg Line at points in between. French General Foch was the over-all commander.

The big push into the Argonne started on September 26. The forest was one of the most ancient wooded areas in France. Charlemagne had hunted stags and bears in its deep recesses more than a thousand years before. In 1917, it was still a tangled mass of thick woods covering a broken, hilly terrain. But the Germans had nearly every square foot of it fortified.

The Yanks found it tough going. Thousands of brave men died for every mile the A.E.F. advanced, and the field hospitals

Surrendering German soldiers are led away by their Allied captors.

A funeral service on the battlefield for one of the many American casualties.

were filled to overflowing. But Pershing's men doggedly pressed on. It was in the heart of the gloomy Argonne Forest that one of the great adventures in American military history took place.

The 1st Battalion of the 77th Division ("New York's Own") had been assigned to go forward to take a certain ridge. As they moved through the wet, silent woods, they could hear firing on both sides. Suddenly, without warning, they were surrounded by Germans. Quickly, the men dug a shallow circular trench and dropped inside. They began to return the fire from German rifles and machine guns that was pouring in on them from everywhere.

Major Charles W. Whittlesey, the commanding officer, sent messages for help by carrier pigeon. But it didn't come. The Yanks were

The first contact between the German Army and American troops occurred June 3, 1918. The advancing Germans had forced the French to retreat and give up Belleau Wood. The Germans stormed through the waist-high wheat in hot pursuit of the French when they were abruptly halted. The line of American Marines that had been quickly brought into action held.

running out of ammunition. Under a flag of truce, the Germans sent a message urging the men to surrender for humanity's sake. The Yanks refused. Airplanes tried to drop food and ammunition, but the packages, falling outside the armed circle, were seized by the Germans.

Amid the pounding of heavy artillery, mortar shells, machine guns, grenades, and rifle fire, the Lost Battalion managed somehow to hang on. On the fifth day, they were rescued. Seven hundred men went in with Major Whittlesey; less than 200 came out. The Lost Battalion became an American legend.

It was in the Argonne, too, that Alvin York, a farm boy from the hills of Tennessee, became one of the greatest heroes of the war. Leading a patrol through the thick woods, York accidentally got inside the enemy lines. When a machine gun opened up on the patrol, York quickly put it out of action with his rifle. (He had been the turkey-shooting champion back home.) Germans came out of the woods from all sides with their hands up. By the time he got back to his own lines, Alvin York was marching a veritable army of prisoners in front of his gun—128 men and four officers!

THE ARMISTICE

By November 1, 1918, Pershing's men had fought their way through the Argonne to the other side. Now, they were advancing by leaps and bounds. To the north, Haig's British and French had shattered their part of the Hindenburg Line. The once-proud German Army was rapidly collapsing, and their fairly orderly retreat turning into a rout. On September 29, 1918, Ludendorff declared that further resistance was impossible; he advised the German Government to ask for an armistice. The new German Chancellor, Prince Max von Baden, followed his advice and began armistice negotiations.

Back in Germany, the people on the home front were just as undone as the soldiers on the battle front. There was little or no food except potatoes and turnips. Germany had been fighting half a world virtually alone, and the dreaded casualty lists—practically every family had lost a father, son, or husband—had made the people sick to death of war. Even defeat was better than the life they had been living for over a year.

On November 10th, the Kaiser and his family fled to exile in Holland. And the next day, at 11 A.M., November 11, 1918, the last shot of the war was fired. A dead quiet settled over the Western Front. In a few weeks, birds began to sing again in the shattered trees.

Ironically, in Russia, Allied soldiers, including Americans, fought on for nine months after the Armistice was signed.

By November 4, all of Germany's allies, Austria-Hungary, Bulgaria, and Turkey had surrendered, Emperor Francis Joseph had died in 1916 to be followed to the throne of the Austro-Hungarian Monarchy by Charles IV. By the summer of 1918, the Hapsburg Monarchy was well on its way to dissolution. Uprisings were common in all the territories, and men were deserting the army on a large scale. Provisional Czech, Polish, and Yugoslav Governments were formed and legions of their soldiers were fighting on the side of the Allies. The armistice which was negotiated on November 3, 1918, marked the end of the Monarchy and the Empire. The Hungarian, Czech, Polish, and Yugoslavian provinces proclaimed their independence, and on November 13, the Republic of Austria was established.

The League of Nations

President Wilson called the war "a war to make the world safe for democracy." The people of the world took heart. Perhaps, this bloody holocaust had indeed been "the war to end all wars." In January of 1918, he announced America's plans for permanent peace, which became famous as "the Fourteen Points." They outlined:

1. Abolition of secret treaties.
2. Freedom of the seas.
3. Removal of trade barriers between nations.
4. Reduction of arms.
5. Adjustment of colonial claims.
6. Restoration of Russian territory.
7. Restoration of Belgian territory.
8. Return of Alsace-Lorraine to France.
9. Readjustment of Italian frontiers.
10. Freedom for the people of Austria-Hungary.
11. Freedom for the Balkans.
12. Freedom for the people conquered by Turkey.
13. Establishment of an independent Poland.
14. Creation of a League of Nations.

Wilson dreamed of a war-free world. He did not wish to punish Germany for starting the war. But Prime Minister Lloyd George of England and Premier Georges Clemenceau of France had different ideas. Their countries had been badly hurt by German aggression, and they wanted revenge.

At the Peace Conference at Versailles on June 28, 1919 — just five years to the day after Gavrilo Princip fired his fatal shot—the leaders of England and France, over Wilson's protests, imposed harsh and humiliating punishment on Germany in the way of loss of territory and reparations.

Ironically, the United States was the only major nation that refused to join the League. The American people were tired of war, and fed up with Europe's problems. They wanted to get back to "good old American normalcy."

The League of Nations faltered along from its beginning, and just before the outbreak of World War II, it died. But out of Woodrow Wilson's great dream grew the idea of our present United Nations, depended on by people the world over to keep the peace.

What Did the War Cost— in Lives and Money?

The worst loss that nations suffer in war is in loss of lives.

It is estimated that the death toll among soldiers in World War I rose to 12,991,000.

To this frightful figure must be added an estimated 10,000,000 civilian dead from famine, disease, and privation caused by the war.

In addition, more than 21,219,000 soldiers were wounded, many of these men incapacitated for life.

In dollars and cents, the cost of the war has been reliably fixed at $337,980,579,657. (This figure includes military supplies, shipping losses, property damage, and losses in production.) We are still paying the bill.

What a terrible price the whole world had to pay for the ambitions of a handful of men greedy for power and prestige.

Highlights of World War I

Declarations of War —1914-1918

1914
July 28 — Austria on Serbia.
Aug. 1 — Germany on Russia.
Aug. 3 — Germany on France.
Aug. 4 — Germany on Belgium.
England on Germany.
Aug. 5 — Montenegro on Austria.
Aug. 6 — Austria on Russia.
Serbia on Germany.
Aug. 8 — Montenegro on Germany.
Aug. 12 — France on Austria.
England on Austria.
Aug. 23 — Japan on Germany.
Aug. 25 — Japan on Austria.
Aug. 28 — Austria on Belgium.
Nov. 2 — Russia on Turkey.
Serbia on Turkey.
Nov. 5 — England on Turkey.
France on Turkey.

1915
May 23 — Italy on Austria.
June 3 — San Marino on Austria.
Aug. 21 — Italy on Turkey.
Oct. 14 — Bulgaria on Serbia.
Oct. 15 — England on Bulgaria.
Montenegro on Bulgaria.
Oct. 16 — France on Bulgaria.
Oct. 19 — Russia on Bulgaria.
Italy on Bulgaria.

1916
Mar. 9 — Germany on Portugal.
Mar. 15 — Austria on Portugal.
Aug. 27 — Rumania on Austria.
Aug. 28 — Italy on Germany.
Germany on Rumania.
Aug. 30 — Turkey on Rumania.
Sept. 1 — Bulgaria on Rumania.

1917
Apr. 6 — United States on Germany.

Apr. 7 — Cuba on Germany.
Panama on Germany.
June 27 — Greece on Germany, Austria, Turkey, and Bulgaria.
July 22 — Siam on Germany and Austria.
Aug. 4 — Liberia on Germany.
Aug. 14 — China on Germany and Austria.
Oct. 26 — Brazil on Germany.
Dec. 7 — United States on Austria.
Dec. 10 — Panama on Austria.
Dec. 16 — Cuba on Austria.

1918
Apr. 23 — Guatemala on Germany.
May 8 — Nicaragua on Germany and Austria.
May 23 — Costa Rica on Germany.
July 12 — Haiti on Germany.
July 19 — Honduras on Germany.

The Fighting —1914-1918

1914
Aug. 4 German Army invades Belgium.
Aug. 7 Russian Army invades East Prussia.
Aug. 20 Germans occupy Brussels. First German air raid on Paris.
Aug. 22 Germans invade France.
Aug. 23 Japanese forces attack German colony at Kai-chau.
Aug. 26-31 Russians defeated at Battle of Tannenberg.
Aug. 28 British cruisers raid German naval base at Heligoland; are driven off.
Sept. 1 French Army defeated at Soissons; begins retreat through France.
Sept. 3 French Government moves from Paris to Bordeaux.
Sept. 6 Battle of the Marne begins.
Sept. 6-15 Russians defeated at Battle of Masurian Lakes.
Sept. 10 French repel Germans at Marne.

Sept. 12 Beginning of trench warfare.
Oct. 5 Germans advance on Warsaw.
Oct. 25 Attack on Warsaw fails.
Nov. 7 Kai-chau surrenders to Japanese. (At about this same time, Japanese forces occupied the German Pacific Islands: Marshalls, Mariannas, Carolines, Palaw.)
Nov. 17 Germans repulsed at Ypres.
Dec. 14-24 British attack on Nieuport-Verdun line bogs down.
Dec. 24-25 British Air Force raids German positions in Belgium.

1915
Jan. 8 Germans make slight gains against Allied lines at Soissons.
Jan. 31 Germans renew attack on Warsaw.
Feb. 12 German Army invades Russia.
Feb. 19 Allied naval squadrons bombard Dardenelles; are repulsed.
Feb. 26 Heavy fighting at Champagne; the battle is a stand-off.

Mar. 20 Zeppelin raids on Paris.
Apr. 22 Second Battle of Ypres; Germans introduce poisonous gas.
Apr. 25 British and ANZAC troops land at Gallipoli.
May 1 Turks attack British beachheads at Gallipoli.
May 7 *Lusitania* sunk by German U-boat.
May 9-June 18 Second battle of Champagne; no gain for either side.
May 23 Austrians attack Italian forces.
May 25 Winston Churchill resigns as First Lord of British Admiralty.
May 26-31 Zeppelin raids on London.
June 21-July 1 Heavy fighting at Gallipoli.
July 1 Heavy fighting in Argonne sector.
July 15 Conquest of German South Africa completed.
Aug. 5 Germans take Warsaw.
Aug. 12-Sept. 8 Severe Zeppelin raids on London.

145

Sept. 23 Big Allied offensive opens on Western Front.

Oct. 2 Worst Zeppelin raids to date on London.

Oct. 13 English nurse Edith Cavell shot as spy by Germans.

Dec. 7 Seige of Kut-al-Imara by Turks.

Dec. 8 British begin retreat from Gallipoli.

1916

Jan. 19 Gallipoli evacuated by British and ANZAC forces.

Jan. 29-31 Zeppelin raids on Paris and London.

Feb. 2 Heavy fighting between Austrians and Russians.

Feb. 21 German attack on Verdun begins.

Mar. 25 British destroyers and planes raid Zeppelin hangers at Schleswig.

March 30 British hospital ship sunk by Turks in Black Sea.

Apr. 10 Germans gain at Verdun.

Apr. 29 British forces at Kut surrender.

May 15 Heavy fighting at Vimy Ridge.

May 31-June 1 Battle of Jutland.

June 5 Austrians advance in Italy.

June 16 Germans advance to within four miles of Verdun.

July 1 Battle of Somme begins; First use of British tanks.

Sept. 12 French advance on the Somme.

Oct. 7 German submarine U-53 reaches Newport, R.I.

Oct. 8 U-53 torpedoes five ships off Nantucket.

Oct. 22 Russians defeated in Galicia.

Nov. 18 Battle of Somme ends.

Nov. 21 Emperor Franz Joseph of Austria-Hungary dies.

Nov. 28 First German airplane raid on London.

Dec. 10 German commercial submarine, *Deutschland,* completes second voyage to United States.

Dec. 15 French drive Germans back, win victory at Verdun.

1917

Jan. 8 German High Command decides on unrestricted submarine warfare.

Jan. 19 Von Zimmerman note to Mexican Ambassador urging a Mexican alliance with Germany against the U.S.

Jan. 31 Germany notifies U.S. that unrestricted U-boat warfare will begin Feb. 1.

Feb. 3 U.S. severs relations with Germany.

March 8 Russian Revolution begins.

March 11 Baghdad occupied by British forces.

March 15 Czarist Government overthrown in Russia.

April 3 Germans retreat to Hindenberg Line after massive British and French attacks.

April 6 U.S. declares war on Germany.

Apr. 9 Battle of Arras begins; British take Vimy Ridge.

Apr. 16-20 Second battle of Aisne; British and French suffer heavy losses.

June First U.S. troops land in France, General Pershing commanding.

June 7 British launch mass surprise attack on Messines Ridge.

June 31-Nov. 10 Third Battle of Ypres; British troops gain about five miles at a cost of 400,000 men.

July Lawrence of Arabia emerges as legendary hero of the war in the desert.

Aug. 20-Dec. 15 Second Battle of Verdun.

Oct. 24 Italian line shattered by German-Austrian forces at Caporetto; Italians retreat in confusion.

Nov. 8 Bolsheviks overthrow revolutionary Russian Government under Kerensky.

Nov. 20-Dec. 3 Battle of Cambrai; British attack with 380 tanks, but are unable to follow their advantage.

Dec. 5 British withdraw from Cambrai.

Dec. 8 British conquer German East Africa.

Dec. 9 General Allenby takes Jerusalem.

1918

Jan. 6 Armistice between Germany and Russia.

Jan. 7 German sailors mutiny at Kiel.

Jan. 10 Russian Black Sea fleet mutinies.

Mar. 3 Peace treaty of Brest-Litovsk between Russia and Central Powers.

Mar. 21 German spring offensive begins on Western front; British forces driven back at Ypres and Amiens.

Apr. 5 British and Japanese Marines land at Vladivostok.

Apr. 11 Germans take Armentières.

Apr. 22 British navy raids Zeebrugge and Ostend.

May 7 Peace treaty between Germany and Rumania.

May 29 Germans take Soissons.

June 1 German offensive reaches Château-Thierry.

June 4 U.S. divisions help drive Germans back across the Marne.

June 11 Allied counteroffensive stops German advance.

July 10 French at Marne.

July 19 American cruiser, *San Diego,* sunk off Fire Island, N. Y.

July 21 Americans and French take Château-Thierry.

Aug. 7 German sailors mutiny at Wilhelmshaven.

Aug. 30 Germans retreat in Flanders.

Sept. 1 British advance in Macedonia.

Sept. 3 Germans retreat to the Somme.

Sept. 22 Allenby advances in Palestine.

Sept. 26 Americans and French launch Argonne attack.

Sept. 27 American Army provides vital strength that breaks the Hindenberg Line.

Sept. 29 Bulgaria surrenders.

Oct. 6 Americans take St. Etienne and La Château.

First peace note sent by German Government to President Wilson.

Oct. 9 Allies retake Cambrai.

Oct. 12 Germans send second peace note to U.S. President.

Oct. 14 President Wilson replies; says peace terms must be left to military leaders, Germans must change their Government.

Oct. 17 Allies retake Ostend, Bruges, and Lille.

Oct. 30 Turkey surrenders.

Nov. 4 Austria surrenders.

Nov. 7 Americans take Sedan; break backbone of German resistance.

Nov. 10 Emperor Wilhelm flees to Holland.

Nov. 11 Germany signs armistice; Firing ceases at 11 A.M.

Nov. 21 German Navy surrenders to British.

Nov. 25 Last remnants of German forces in East Africa surrender.

Dec. 6 American occupation troops enter Germany.

1919

Jan. 10 Austria signs peace treaty at Paris.

June 28 Germans sign Treaty of Versailles.

1920

Jan. 10 League of Nations formed.

THE
SECOND WORLD WAR

FRANCE

GERMANY

ITALY

ENGLAND

RUSSIA

JAPAN

CHINA

U.S.A.

MUSSOLINI

The Years Before the War

In the spring of 1939, the whole world was sitting on a gigantic powder keg that was all set to explode. The fuse, in fact, had already been lighted in a dozen places. It was burning slowly but surely. Sooner or later, the explosion was certain to come. It was only a matter of time.

Why was the world about to plunge into a terrible war that would cost millions of human lives and hundreds of billions of dollars? To find the answer, we must first take a brief look at what was going on in Italy, Germany, Japan, England, France, Russia, and the United States.

After the close of World War I (1914-1918), the leading nations of the world had agreed that, in the future, all international disputes would be settled by peaceful means. They pledged never to engage in another war.

But in the years that followed, the leaders of three nations — Germany, Italy, and Japan — were not willing to live up to this idealistic agreement. They openly desired some of the lands and resources of neighboring countries and secretly planned to take them by force of arms.

In Italy, in 1922, Benito Mussolini had taken over control of the

HITLER

HIROHITO

The barefoot Ethiopians were gallant fighters, but no match for the Italian tanks in 1935.

government from a weakling king. Although he allowed the King, Victor Emmanuel, to stay on as a figurehead, Mussolini made himself the supreme dictator. As the head of his all-powerful political party, the Fascists, he rewrote all the laws to suit himself. He dreamed of turning Italy once more into a great empire, as it had been in the days of the ancient Romans.

Mussolini began to put his schemes of conquest into action in 1935 by invading and conquering the small and primitive African kingdom of Ethiopia. The barefoot Ethiopians, armed only with spears and a few outdated guns, were no match for the Italian tanks and bombing planes. Within a few weeks, Ethiopia was an Italian colony, and Mussolini was planning further conquests.

At about this same time, in Germany, Adolph Hitler made himself dictator of that country. After World War I, all of Germany's overseas possessions had been taken away. She had been required to make payment of money and materials as reparations, or compensation, for the losses suffered by the victors. Her boundaries had been revised and her armed forces limited to prevent future aggression.

Hitler promised that he and his followers, called Nazis, would change all this. He was determined to build Germany once again into a great

149

world power. His plan, at first, was to conquer all of Europe and create a "greater Germany" that, in his own words, would endure for a thousand years. In Hitler's sick, mad mind, he was already dreaming of world conquest, a world in which Germany would be the leading power on earth. The German people, he thought, were the "master race" and all other peoples were inferior.

Great segments of the population, disillusioned at the widespread unemployment, an unstable economy, and bitter over their losses in World War I, found encouragement in Hitler's wild speeches. Democratic Germans, opposed to the dictator's program, were either killed, imprisoned, or forced to escape the country.

In defiance of the peace treaty that followed World War I, Hitler began building up Germany's armed forces. When they were strong enough, he started to carry out his grand plan for European conquest.

While these events were going on in Italy and Germany, France was trying to rebuild herself out of the ruins of the war. Although the French had been victorious in World War I, most of the battles had been fought on their own soil and much of their land had been devastated. The French, though concerned, were too busy to pay much serious attention to what was happening across the Rhine in Germany or south of the Alps in Italy.

The English also did not seem to be fully aware of the storm that was brewing. They had the world's greatest navy, and were confident that no enemy could invade their island country. They saw what Hitler and Mussolini were doing, but they had other things on their minds. Chief among these was the rebuilding of their worldwide trade, which had all but collapsed while they were fighting, and helping to win, the First World War. England refused to believe that another world war could happen.

Meanwhile, the vast land of Russia was in the process of recovering from the bloodiest revolution in history, which had broken out in 1917. In this revolution, the Communists had seized the reins of government from the Czars. Eventually, a revolutionary leader, Josef Stalin, emerged as dictator. The Communists planned, first, to make their own country strong. When that had been done, they intended to expand their Communistic form of government all over the rest of the world. Like Italy and Germany, the Russians were building up a powerful army and air force.

But the Russians were working quietly, and most of the world paid little attention to them. Russia had always been a big, but backward, country; and the leaders of the other nations blindly assumed that it always would be.

The fuse was also burning on the Pacific side of the world. The Japanese Empire had emerged as a world power after its defeat of Russia in 1905. Now it was planning the conquest of all Asia. This would include about one-half of the world's population and a large portion of its natural resources. The Japanese people believed that their Emperor was descended from the sun goddess, and that is was his divine mission to rule the world.

The Japanese had begun their plan of conquest before either Italy or Germany. In 1931, they invaded the Chinese province of Manchuria and set up a puppet state called Manchukuo. In 1937, with China torn by civil war, they invaded the remainder of the country. The Japanese, in the spring of 1939, were already well on their way to their dream of glory.

In the United States, two factors were at work that prevented Americans from paying much heed to the prophetic events that were happening in other parts of the world.

One of these was the fact that the nation was just recovering from the great depression of 1929, when many people were unable to find jobs and many businesses had failed. Americans were chiefly concerned with recovering their former prosperity.

The second of these factors, and perhaps the more important one, was that most of the American political leaders believed that the United States should not become entangled in the affairs of foreign governments. "America is protected by two great oceans," they said in effect, "the Atlantic on one side and the Pacific on the other. Let the nations of Europe and Asia fight among themselves if they want to. We will remain at peace."

So England, France, and the United States were too involved in their own affairs to become very alarmed at the plans for world conquest that were being hatched in Italy, Germany, Russia, and Japan.

The fuse was burning short, and the powder keg was ready to blow up.

The Coming Storm

Both Italy and Japan had already set their machines of conquest in motion. Now Germany joined the game. Hitler found an excuse for his moves of aggression in the terms of the peace treaty that had ended World War I, or simply denounced them.

His first move was to scrap the World War I agreements that limited Germany's armed forces. Then he sent his army into the Rhineland, the border region with France. According to treaty, this area was to remain demilitarized; that is, free of troops and military fortifications. Now France was suddenly faced with German soldiers at her border. Surprised, unprepared to fight, and wishing to avoid open conflict, the French did nothing to stop Hitler.

Then Hitler and Mussolini signed a mutual-aid pact that was known as the Rome-Berlin Axis. The European nations openly began to choose up sides.

On September 1, 1939, Germany invaded Poland. World War II had begun.

For some years, Hitler had been building the Nazi party in Austria. Now, with the support of many Austrians, he marched his troops into that country. The German Army took over the Austrian Government, which had been forced to resign, and Hitler announced that Austria was a part of the German nation. This union, or *Anschluss*, was in violation of the World War I peace treaty, which had forbidden a union with Austria.

At the World War I peace conference, many of the old boundaries in central Europe had been changed, and a number of new nations had been created out of the old Austro-Hungarian Empire. The treaty makers had affirmed that the people of these regions had a right to determine for themselves the form of government under which they would live. Now Hitler turned this principle of "self-determination" to his own purposes.

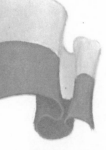

POLISH FLAG

He declared that many German people were being forced against their will to live in a certain part of Czechoslovakia, and that it was the duty of the German Government to liberate them. Hitler then declared his intention of annexing this part of Czechoslovakia, known as the Sudetenland, in which a large number of German-speaking people lived, and in which he had also been building up the Nazi party. At this, the English at last became alarmed. It looked as though Hitler was going to gobble up all of central Europe without any opposition. But Great Britain, like France, was not prepared for war, and was willing to do almost anything to avoid it.

The Prime Minister of Great Britain, Neville Chamberlain, and the Premier of France, Edouard Daladier, went to Germany to confer with Hitler about the Sudetenland problem. At their famous meeting in Munich, Hitler promised that the Sudetenland would be the last piece of European territory he would demand. The British and French leaders agreed, and Prime Minister Chamberlain went back to England proclaiming that the Munich Pact assured "peace in our time."

The Prime Minister was hardly back in England when Hitler marched his army into the Sudetenland — and then, later, seized the rest of Czechoslovakia as well.

In Italy, the armies of Mussolini invaded and conquered the little Balkan country of Albania. At about the same time, Hitler began to make demands upon Poland for certain territory that had once been a part of Germany.

Now the powder keg could go up in smoke and flames any minute. Although sadly unprepared, both France and Great Britain signed agreements with Poland to give her military help in case the Germans should attack. At the same time, they urged the Poles to avoid any act against Germany that might appear to be warlike.

The British and French had hoped to bring Russia into an alliance with themselves against the Rome-Berlin Axis. But, without warning, the Russians suddenly signed a non-aggression pact with Germany. By its terms, each agreed not to take up arms against the other in case a European war burst into flames.

Both countries had selfish reasons for such a pact. Germany wanted to keep Russia off the side of England and France. The Russians wanted to strengthen their own defenses against Germany, and not get involved with the trouble that seemed to be brewing in Poland.

At this time, in the late summer of 1939, the German land forces numbered about 2 1/2 million men. They were then the best-equipped, best-trained soldiers in the world.

Hitler was at last ready for his big war of conquest. He started the ball rolling by announcing that Polish troops had fired on German troops. Of course, this was a lie, but Hitler wanted an excuse to attack. The fact that he had to make it up himself didn't bother him. He declared that if these "attacks" went on, he would march his army into Poland in order to defend Germany. Then, early in the morning of September 1, 1939, the German Army crossed the Polish border. World War II had begun.

The Poles had an army that was almost as large as the Germans'. But they were sadly lacking in the weapons of modern warfare. They were hopelessly outclassed in terms of tanks, airplanes, and heavy guns. In the air, Poland was outnumbered, 10 or 12 to 1; and their planes, which were mostly old-fashioned models, were no match for the efficient German bombers.

On that morning of September 1, the German Army, or *Wehrmacht* as it was called, and the German Air Force, or *Luftwaffe*, struck Poland with a lightning blow. Hitler's generals had planned the attack well. The dive-bombers flew in first, blasting the countryside underneath them. Then the columns of German tanks slammed into the Polish defenses like a battering ram.

Most of Poland's air force was destroyed before its planes could get off the ground. And most of the army was surrounded and crushed before it had a chance to take up defensive positions. At the same time, the *Luftwaffe* dive-bombers pulverized Warsaw, Poland's capital city, with the first large-scale, all-out raid in history.

The brave Poles did not give up without a struggle. But that struggle was doomed to defeat before it started. The cream of the Polish Army was horse cavalry, and they made a gallant attempt to resist. But men on horses have no chance against men in airplanes and tanks. One by one, these pockets of defenders were wiped out by the advancing Germans.

The pilots of German scouting planes could see every move that the Poles were making. On the other hand, having no airplanes left, the Poles had no way of knowing where the German invaders would strike next. The horsemen of the Polish cavalry were ineffective as scouting units.

By the end of the first week, the war was as good as over. The Polish Army was broken up into scattered units of resistance, which the Germans were crushing piecemeal. At the end of the third week, virtually all fighting had stopped.

On September 17, the Russian Army moved into Poland, and on the 28th, Russia and Germany divided that unhappy country between them. Poland no longer existed as a nation. The first stage of World War II was finished almost before the rest of the startled world realized that it had begun.

A Polish Government-in-exile was formed in England, however, and Polish units attached to the British armed forces took part in the Allied offensive against Germany.

The French and the Germans faced each other from behind the Maginot and Siegfried Lines. The border between France and neutral Belgium was guarded by British Expeditionary Forces and French units.

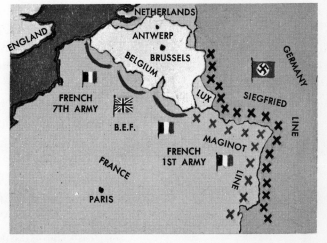

The "Quiet" Western Front

On September 3, two days after Hitler's attack on Poland, both Great Britain and France honored their agreements by declaring war upon Germany. But then a curious thing happened. Neither of them made any attempt to go to Poland's aid.

Instead, a few British divisions landed in France and took up positions behind the Maginot Line. This was a strong line of fortifications that had been built during the period between the two World Wars. It extended all the way along the border that separated France and Germany.

The French assumed that any future war would be fought from fixed positions and lines of trenches and fortifications like those of World

155

War I. And so they and the British felt secure behind these mighty forts. Both countries began to build up their armies while they sat behind the Maginot Line and waited for the Germans to attack. But the preparations proceeded slowly.

The Germans, on the other hand, had no intention of fighting a static war. They were not going to try a frontal attack on the powerful Maginot Line. Instead, they planned to swing their columns of tanks and marching men around the northern end of the Maginot Line, through Belgium, Holland, and Luxembourg, and fall upon the Allied defenses from behind. The Maginot guns, firmly embedded in the steel and concrete of the massive forts, could be fired only in the direction of Germany. They could not be turned around, and were therefore useless against an assault from the rear.

The original war plan of the German High Command had been to attack in October, two weeks after the surrender of the Poles. But the campaign in Poland had taught them that good weather for their tanks and bombers was essential to the kind of "lightning war" they intended to employ. However, the weather forecasts were not as favorable as the German generals considered necessary for a quick victory, and the attack was postponed.

After two more postponements, the assault was finally put off until the spring of 1940. So, all winter long, the Allies, as the French and British were called, sat behind their fortifications and did little or nothing This period was labeled the "phony war."

Meanwhile, the Russians, who had taken a part of Poland after the German victory there, made a surprise attack of their own against Finland, their tiny neighbor to the northwest. After their seizure of Polish territory, the Russians had demanded military bases in Estonia, Latvia, Lithuania, and Finland. The first three of these little nations agreed, much against their wills. But the independent-minded Finns flatly refused. Therefore, on November 30, 1939, Russian planes staged an air raid on Helsinki, the Finnish capital. A few days later, Russian divisions swarmed across the border.

But the Russians did not find the going in Finland as easy as the Germans had found it in Poland. In the first place, the Finnish Army, though small, was superbly trained. Secondly, the Russians attacked in the middle of t he sub-Arctic winter. The Finns fought on skis, and the Russians bogged down in the deep snows. Russian planes began a systematic bombing of Finnish cities and communication centers, but flying conditions were bad and the damage was not great.

During the grueling battle in the fjord at Narvik, two British destroyers and 10 German ships were lost.

After invading Denmark, the Germans landed at six different points on the coast of Norway (red arrows). The British (blue) sent help, but in vain.

NARVIK

FINLAND

NAMSOS

SWEDEN

TRONDHEIM

ANDALSNES

NORWAY

OSLO

BERGEN

STAVANGER

KRISTIANSAND

KATTEGAT

DENMARK

NORTH SEA

BALTIC SEA

Fighting in the Finnish forests, in the deep snow, Russian losses were extremely high. But their numbers in tanks and men were so superior that the Finns, although still fighting fiercely, could not stand up against the Russians. When spring approached, and the snows began to melt, the gallant little Finnish Army was melting away just as rapidly.

The Finnish Army was led by General Carl von Mannerheim, who was to become President of Finland in 1944.

In March, the Finns were finally forced to give up. Russia took a large part of southern Finland as spoils of war, and established political domination over the remainder.

The Invasion of Scandinavia

Skis were a valuable means of transportation during the Finno-Russian War.

During the winter of 1939-1940, while all was quiet in the "phony war" along the Western Front, the German generals decided to attack and occupy Denmark and Norway. Their object was to establish air bases and naval bases for the attack that they planned to make against Great Britain.

Therefore, early on the morning of April 9, 1940, the *Wehrmacht* began to move in on both these peaceful Scandinavian countries. The Danes and Norwegians were taken completely off guard.

Denmark had only a very small air force and army. As the Germans marched in, large flights of *Luftwaffe* bombers thundered over all principal Danish cities to frighten the government and the people. They dropped no bombs, but it was obvious to the terrified citizens on the ground below that the Germans could, and would, drop bombs if any move was made to stop them.

In a few places, isolated units of the Danish Army tried to resist the German columns, but they were quickly wiped out. The Germans said that they had not come as enemies, but only to protect the Danes against an Allied attack.

During the occupation, the Danish underground movement conducted a highly effective resistance. Its work in sabotaging the German war effort was so widespread and so successful, that a vast number of German soldiers were required to occupy the country.

Like Denmark, Norway was virtually helpless against attack. In addition, the Germans had laid their plans well ahead of time and with great care. A Norwegian politician named Vidkun Quisling, who had formerly been Secretary of War, was a Nazi and thus a German sympathizer. He had agreed to see to it that such little defenses as the Norwegians had would be disrupted when the sneak attack came.

Consequently, when German troopships steamed into Norwegian harbors at several strategic points, the little Norwegian Army found itself almost totally unprepared, thanks to the work of Quisling and the disloyal officers who were in the plot with him. These traitors had also informed the Germans of the location of all Norwegian arms and supplies, which further hampered the nation's defense.

But the forts along the coast put up a determined fight, and despite the heavy odds against them, the brave Norwegians succeeded in sinking three German cruisers.

The Allies immediately mounted a counter-invasion against the Germans in Norway. On April 13, a force of about 20,000 British Tommies — including a scattering of French and Poles — landed at several points on the Norwegian coast. Their intention was to reconquer Norway before the Germans could get organized to hold it.

"Now," people said to each other, "the Germans will find out what it is like to go up against real soldiers instead of helpless civilians."

But, unfortunately, the British were not soldiers of the regular army. They were Territorials, military units of Great Britain's home defense forces. They were not well-trained nor well-armed. On the other hand, the German units had been hand-picked from the best of the *Wehrmacht's* crack mountain troops.

Furthermore, the Germans by then were in almost full control of all Norwegian seaports, and the Allied army was unable to land tanks, artillery, and other heavy fighting equipment. As if that fact were not handicap enough, the Territorials had no air cover. They were completely at the mercy of the *Luftwaffe,* and took a furious and constant pounding from German bombers. In addition, they were out-maneuvered and out-fought on the ground.

The British hung on for about a month. Then it became apparent that there was no use in continuing a hopeless struggle. All of their scattered units withdrew except one that had captured the northern port of Narvik.

Then came the surprise German attack against Belgium, Holland, and France in early May, and these last British units evacuated Narvik and managed to get back to England.

Thus the first clash between Allied and German armies ended in

General Mannerheim led the Finnish Army in a gallant but losing war against superior Russian arms and manpower.

disaster for the Allies. It was going to be one in a long series of such disasters that would last for the next two years.

Soon, German units had spread all through Norway, and had the entire country firmly under control. The Germans later named Vidkun Quisling head of the puppet government that they created to rule Norway, and he continued to carry out their orders during the rest of the German occupation.

But all through the German occupation, a small but fierce undercover army of loyal Norwegians continued to fight the invaders, blowing up Nazi supply centers and other installations. Thousands of other Norwegians, who had escaped the Nazis, fought bravely with the Allies in Europe.

About 335,000 Allied forces succeeded in withdrawing from Dunkirk in northern France across the English Channel to England.

Quisling was executed before a Norwegian firing squad for his crimes at the war's end in 1945. On that shameful morning of April 9, 1940, a new word entered the language of all the freedom-loving peoples of the world. The word was *quisling*, meaning "traitor."

After the Norwegian defeat, Neville Chamberlain resigned in disgrace as Prime Minister of Great Britain, and that great wartime leader, Winston Churchill, succeeded him to pull the British together and give them courage for the long struggle that lay ahead.

The Germans Break Through

Early in the morning of May 10, 1940, the waiting German Army struck out at France. According to their preconceived plan, they did not try to break through the powerful Maginot Line, but instead swooped around it to the north through Holland, Belgium, and Luxembourg.

These little countries were woefully unprepared when the massive German Army — consisting of 150 full combat divisions, 10,000 tanks, and 5,000 planes — hit them a massive blow without warning. In fact, the Army of Luxembourg consisted of only 300 soldiers and a handful of police.

Holland relied for her defense chiefly on the fact that much of the land lies below sea level and must be protected by dikes. Elaborate plans had been made to flood the land in the event of an invasion, so that German tanks would be unable to move in the mud.

Before dawn, *Luftwaffe* bombers hit all the important Dutch airfields and knocked out the tiny Dutch Air Force. They also destroyed many of the larger Dutch cities, slaughtering thousands of helpless civilians.

The bombers were followed by flights of cargo planes that carried parachutists. Like Quisling and his followers in Norway, there were many Nazis in Holland. These Dutch traitors knew that the Germans were coming and were waiting to help them. Together, these traitors and Hitler's airborne troops quickly destroyed all the vital centers of communication and foiled the plan for flooding the country.

The bulk of the German Army then came in over roads that were perfectly dry, and they occupied the country. A squad of parachutists made an attempt to kidnap Queen Wilhelmina, but she and her family managed to escape to England. There the Queen established a Government-in-exile, as did all the other conquered countries.

The Dutch had flooded eastern areas of their country as a defense against German attack. But the Nazis invaded Holland from the south and also parachuted soldiers and heavy equipment into the country.

Without trying to storm the Maginot Line, the German Army outflanked the Allied forces by invading Holland and Belgium and cutting the Allies off from the coast.

Four days after the first attack, all of Holland was in German hands.

At the same hour that the Germans struck Holland, they also invaded Belgium. This country was much better prepared than Holland, although once more its army was not adequately equipped with tanks, heavy guns, or fighter planes. The Belgians had a defensive line of forts along the German border, but they had made an incredible mistake while building them.

The Belgian Government had contracted with German firms for the construction of many of these forts. The contractors at once turned the plans over to German authorities. In a remote section of Germany, duplicates of the Belgian forts had been built, and parachutists had been trained in methods of destroying them.

In the attack, the Germans employed their usual *blitzkrieg* tactics —a German word meaning "lightning war." The bombers went in first and destroyed cities and airfields. Then came the tanks to wipe out pockets of resistance. After them came the troops. Since the Germans already knew the insides of the forts, they had no trouble taking them.

The German Army kept coming through Belgium and Luxembourg into France. The French and British rushed armies to meet them, but these armies were hopelessly outclassed. Their tanks were very much inferior to those of the *Wehrmacht,* and the Germans destroyed them. The *Luftwaffe* quickly knocked out all the airfields, and soon had complete control of the air.

In a few places, the Allied troops put up gallant fights. But they could not withstand the German tanks and planes. German bombers destroyed the Allied radio and telephone centers, and no one part of the defending army knew where the other parts were. All was confusion.

The Germans swept on with clockwork efficiency. In fact, the tank columns moved so rapidly that they kept well ahead of their supply lines. Since tanks use a great deal of gasoline, there was a danger that the tanks would run dry. But the German commanders gambled that the confused French would make a blunder—which they did. In their haste to retreat, they neglected to remove the gasoline from roadside filling stations. With this vast supply of gas at their disposal, the German tanks kept rolling.

Now, seeing that all was finally lost, the British evacuated their last remaining troops in the north of France to a place called Dunkirk on the English Channel. From here, the British hoped to rescue at least a part of their trapped army.

On the beach, the British soldiers took a terrific mauling from the German tanks and bombers. But miraculously, they managed to hold out until help came. That help took the form of 220 British warships of various sizes and types, and some 650 smaller craft, including pleasure boats and fishing trawlers. (See page 160 for illustration.)

The British Royal Air Force flew over from fields in England to give them air cover and fight off the German bombers. For this operation, the R.A.F. (Royal Air Force), unveiled a new type of fighter plane called the "Spitfire." There were not many of them, but they proved to be vastly superior to the German planes. For the first time in the war, someone had come up with a better weapon than the Germans had.

About 335,000 soldiers made it back to England from Dunkirk. The rest had to be left to their fate. The French continued to fight scattered actions for a few more weeks, but it was clear that they did not have a chance.

One by one, the cities of France fell before the might of the invader. German troops entered Paris on June 14. The French military leader, General Charles de Gaulle, who was in England on a government mission when his country surrendered to Germany, was determined to carry on the fighting in French North Africa. De Gaulle, who was to become President of France after the war, organized the Free French Army to combat the Axis. Like all the resistance armies established by the occupied countries, it was to prove a powerful force for eventual victory.

France surrendered to Hitler on June 24, 1940. Except for the relative handful of men who escaped from Dunkirk, the entire French, Dutch, and Belgian Armies—and the bulk of the British—were lost. Now Germany was triumphant in all of Continental Europe.

On June 10, after the German victory was assured, Mussolini brought Italy into the war as Germany's ally. President Franklin D. Roosevelt, speaking in Washington, called this action a "stab in the back."

Now Japan, although not yet involved in any way with the nations who were fighting in Europe, openly declared its sympathy and support for the German-Italian cause. The Rome-Berlin Axis became the Rome-Berlin-Tokyo Axis.

In October, 1940, Mussolini, who had sent his armies to conquer Albania the year before, invaded Greece. The Greeks at once appealed to Great Britain for aid. Hitler sent troops to help the Italians.

Although the British were already in enough trouble, they sent units of their army and air force into that country. The British forces landed on the island of Crete, as well as on the Greek mainland. They were heavily outnumbered, but they fought like tigers. At last, they were forced to withdraw to the coast, where the British Navy managed to take off about half the survivors. The rest went into hiding in the hills.

The Battle of Britain

After Dunkirk, the new British Prime Minister, Winston Churchill, said: "We shall go on to the end. We shall defend our island whatever the cost may be. We shall fight on the beaches; we shall fight in the streets; we shall fight in the hills. We shall never surrender."

The British people were as brave as their leader; and it is well that they were. For almost all of the remainder of the war, English cities were subjected to frightful bombing raids.

The Battle of Britain, the first one ever fought entirely in the air, began on August 15. The raids continued for more than a month. Sometimes the Germans came over in waves of as many as 2,000 planes. The Spitfires of the R.A.F., although greatly outnumbered by the *Luftwaffe*, were more than a match for them, and inflicted heavy losses on the German invaders.

The Battle of Britain (on opposite page) demanded a superhuman effort from the British military and civilians. Here, German bombers are attacked by Royal Air Force fighters. The inset shows the extent of the damage.

With the "Spitfire," the British had developed a superior fighter plane.

At the same time, British bombers had begun attacking German bases in occupied France, and pounding the boatyards along the Channel coast, where the Germans were building landing craft for their intended invasion across the Channel.

The German planes were attacking at night, with no regard for specific targets. As a result, thousands of civilians were killed and much of London and other cities were destroyed. But the *Luftwaffe* failed to destroy the R.A.F. airfields, and the Spitfires kept coming up to meet the Nazi bombers and shooting them down.

The people of Britain refused to give up, and German plane losses were more than Hitler could take. The *Luftwaffe* discontinued its concentrated attacks, but the ruthless bombing continued on a smaller scale. The Germans had suffered their first defeat.

The map indicates the farthest line reached by the German invaders of Russia. At the height of the invasion, the German supply line extended 1,600 miles.

The Germans Invade Russia

By the early summer of 1941, German engineers had built a huge fleet of landing barges in which the dreaded *Wehrmacht* planned to invade England. The British were braced for the attack, but most neutral observers agreed that they had little, if any, chance of repelling a German invasion in force.

Then, Adolph Hitler did an incredible thing. Instead of attacking England which was lying nearly defenseless across 25 miles of water, he turned his armies eastward and launched an all-out surprise attack on his ally, Russia.

It is known that subduing Russia was a part of his "master plan" of conquest. But why did he do it at this time, against the advice of his generals? Most experts agree that the German dictator had great respect for the British ability to fight back, even though they were then almost helpless after their defeat in France. On the other hand, Hitler held the Russians in complete contempt.

He planned to crush Russia in a "quick campaign" before taking on what he thought would be the much more difficult task of winning the war against England. Of all Hitler's many military mistakes, this one was the most costly.

The attack began on June 22, 1941, with the Germans employing their usual *blitzkrieg* tactics. Thousands of *Luftwaffe* bombers thundered overhead, pounding the Russian defenses. They were followed by the greatest massing of heavy German tanks and mobile artillery yet employed in the war. The brute power of this vast German offensive seemed irresistible.

Caught off guard, the Russians began to fall back. As they retreated, they blew up the bridges and dams, burned the towns, destroyed the grain in the fields.

For the first weeks of the campaign, the German steamroller moved relentlessly ahead, capturing city after city as it moved to its prime objective, Moscow, the Russian capital. Then its tempo began to slow down. The timetable for Hitler's quick victory was upset.

In the first place, the Russian soldiers were better fighters than anyone had imagined. Although vastly outnumbered in guns, tanks, and planes, they fought every step of the way. Then came the rains of late summer, which turned the dirt roads of Russia into rivers of slimy mud. Snow fell earlier than usual in the fall of 1941, slowing down the advance even further.

When the Germans got to the town of Tula, the thunder of the big guns could be heard in Moscow. The Russian Government moved to a city farther east, but the people determined to fight for their capital city.

They didn't have to. Tula was as far as the German offensive got before it was stopped. At the same time, German Armies were stalled on all other parts of the Russian front from Leningrad in the north to Odessa in the south. By early December, the great German Army, hampered by snow and cold weather, could go no farther.

Now, the Russians put the shoe on the other foot. They began a massive counterattack. The Germans dug in on a defensive line and prepared to try to hold what they had taken. The failure of the Russian invasion changed Hitler's war of conquest into a war of defense.

The turning point was the long, drawn-out Battle of Stalingrad—a city that was named after the Russian dictator. (The city has since been renamed Volgograd. Stalin is no longer regarded as a Russian hero.)

Hitler staked the success of his whole Russian campaign on the capture of Stalingrad. He refused to heed the warnings of the members of his general staff, who urged that the wisest move would be to withdraw.

The Russian troops defended the city with deadly determination. The Germans fought their way into the city, house by house. Then, their supply lines, which had been stretched dangerously thin, were cut off. They were stranded at the mercy of their Russian foes.

The German soldiers were starving, freezing, and dying from disease. But for nearly two months more, they managed to hang on in the face of mounting enemy attacks. Then, on January 31, 1943, after more than two years of hammering at the stubborn Russians in quest of a "quick" victory, the German commander surrendered his ragged army of 90,000 men. They were all that were left of the mighty force that had originally marched on the city.

After the defeat at Stalingrad, Hitler's armies never again won another major victory.

The Arsenal of Democracy

At first, the United States had made every effort to avoid taking sides in the war that was raging in Europe. But it quickly became obvious that the war was one between ruthless conquerors on one side and men who wanted to stay free on the other. And, of course, Americans were on the side of freedom.

President Franklin D. Roosevelt put into words what most Americans were thinking. In early 1941, when the British people were fighting with their backs against the wall, he said, "We will give all aid to Britain short of war." This meant that the British would be supplied with tanks, airplanes, guns, and ammunition from American factories.

About that same time, the United States turned 50 destroyers over to the British Navy in return for air and naval bases in Bermuda and other British Islands in the Caribbean Sea.

Great Britain soon exhausted her cash reserves that were in American banks. The United States Congress then passed the Lend-Lease Act. By its terms, the British could buy war supplies in the United States on almost limitless credit.

Now the American industrial economy turned from peacetime production to almost all-out production for war. President Roosevelt said that America would be "the great arsenal of democracy."

In August, 1941, President Roosevelt and Prime Minister Winston Churchill met on board the British battleship *Prince of Wales* in a bay in Newfoundland. Here, they issued a joint document known to history as the Atlantic Charter. In it, the United States and Great Britain pledged that they would work together to keep the spirit of freedom alive in the world.

The United States was not yet actively in the war, but it was dangerously close to the brink.

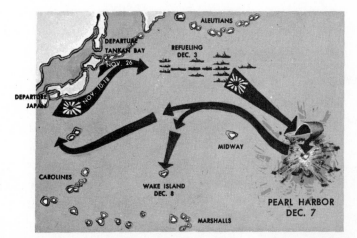

Pearl Harbor

It seemed to the war lords of Japan that now, the autumn of 1941, was the ideal time to put their plan for the conquest of all Asia into action. Germany, which had already defeated Holland and France, as well as other European countries, seemed to be on the verge of doing the same to England and Russia.

Thus, those European countries that held extensive possessions in the Far East would be eliminated, and Japan would have almost a free hand to do as she pleased. Germany could rule the West and Japan could rule the East. Japan could take care of the West later, and eventually rule the world.

The only nation that might upset her plans was the neutral United States. And the only military force that the Japanese had any reason to fear was the United States Pacific Fleet, which was based at Pearl Harbor in Hawaii.

Therefore, they agreed, the first move would be to destroy the Pacific

One month before the surprise air attack on Pearl Harbor, the Japanese task force, which included carriers from which fighter planes would launch their raid, set out from Japan. Returning to port after the attack, they struck at Wake Island.

Fleet. With the fleet gone, it would be a year or more before the United States could fight back over 3,000 miles of ocean. By that time, the Japanese would have completed the conquest of the Philippines, Thailand, Burma, India, the Dutch East Indies, and Australia. Then the United States, alone among the free nations, would have no choice but to ask for a negotiated peace.

In late November, a Japanese striking force of aircraft carriers and escort ships set out across the North Pacific under the cover of winter fog to strike the fatal blow.

On Sunday morning, December 7, 1941, the city of Honolulu and the naval base of Pearl Harbor lay basking in the peaceful tropic sun. The battleships of the Pacific Fleet rolled gently at their moorings.

Then, without warning, at 7:55, the Japanese bombs began to drop. Their first targets were the battleships and the airfields. Within 30 minutes, the job was done. Every one of the battleships had been sunk or put out of commission. The important airfields had been destroyed, along with most of the Army and Marine Corps fighting and bombing planes. The loss in American lives from this sneak attack was appalling.

The next day, December 8, 1941, the Congress of the United States declared war on Japan. Three days later, on December 11, it declared war on the other two Axis powers, Germany and Italy.

Now, at last, the United States was in the war—making it truly a World War. Although the hitting power of the United States Navy had been destroyed, and the American Army was sadly unprepared, Uncle Sam rolled up his sleeves and settled down to the grim task of winning final victory.

The Doolittle Raid

When the United States found itself caught up in the war, the fortunes of the Allies were at their lowest ebb. Poland, Denmark, Norway, Belgium, Luxembourg, Holland, France, Greece, and Yugoslavia had been over-run. Britain was bottled up on its little island. German Armies were deep inside Russia. The United States itself had just suffered the worst naval defeat in history.

After Pearl Harbor, Lieutenant Colonel James C. Doolittle of the Army Air Corps had a bold idea. He proposed to bomb the Japanese

mainland, and even Tokyo itself. Since there were no big bombers with sufficient range to cross the Pacific, he handpicked the crews of 16 B-25 medium Army bombers and trained them to take off from the deck of an aircraft carrier.

On April 18, 1942, the B-25's left the carrier *Hornet* 700 miles off the Japanese coast. They arrived over their objectives without being detected and dropped their bomb loads on Tokyo, Osaka, Yokohama, Kobe, and Nagoya.

Colonel Doolittle's original plan had been to bring the *Hornet* within about 250 miles of Japan before releasing his planes. From this distance, the B-25's would have had enough fuel to accomplish their mission over the Japanese cities and fly on to friendly airfields in China. However, early in the morning, a Japanese trawler was sighted when the *Hornet* was still 700 miles at sea. The trawler was sunk at once by gunfire. But there was no way of knowing whether she had radioed the carrier's position to Japanese headquarters. Colonel Doolittle decided to take no chances. He put his bombers into the air immediately, with himself piloting the lead plane.

Because of the extra 450 miles of flying, none of the B-25's made it to the Chinese airfields. A few crashed, but most were abandoned when they ran out of gas and their crews bailed out. Each of the 16 bombers

The Doolittle raid showed the Japanese war lords that the United States was capable of making direct strikes at Japan.

carried a crew of five. And of these 80 men, 64 (including Doolittle) survived. They were rescued by Chinese patriots and spirited through the Japanese lines to freedom. The raid accomplished little militarily, but it showed the Japanese that they had taken on a foe who was determined, and able, to strike back.

Battle for the Pacific

With its mighty battleships lying on the muddy bottom of Pearl Harbor, and the Japanese fleet in full control of the South Pacific, the United States Navy now turned to the weapon that the Japanese had used so effectively—naval air power.

As quickly as possible, an aircraft carrier task force was assembled and steamed toward the Marshall and Solomon Islands to challenge the navy of the Emperor. It consisted of the carriers *Lexington, Hornet, Yorktown,* and *Enterprise.*

On May 7, 1942, this force detected a Japanese fleet and, in a surprise attack, sank one carrier, in addition to a number of transports and escort vessels. The next day, although the rival task forces were 200 miles apart, another battle took place between carrier-planes and ships. In it, the Japanese lost two carriers, one heavy cruiser, two destroyers, and several smaller ships. But the United States carrier *Lexington* was so badly damaged that she had to be sunk by American gunfire.

The Battle of the Coral Sea, as it was called, was a victory for the United States, and the Japanese fleet returned to its bases to lick its

The map below shows the Battle of the Coral Sea between naval forces of the United States and Japan.

The American attack force headed for Midway is shown, below right, lined up on the deck of the "Enterprise."

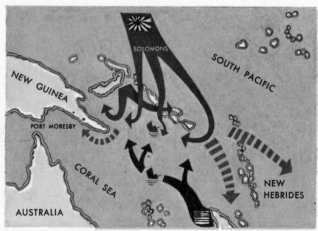

A close-up view of the action
in the fierce Battle of Midway.

An American destroyer
steams to the rescue of the
crew of an American
bomber shot down during
the action.

wounds. This was the first naval battle ever fought in which surface ships did not come in sight of each other.

A month later, American scouting planes reported the Japanese fleet on the move again, this time apparently in full force, but divided into two groups. Altogether they consisted of five carriers, four battleships, eight heavy cruisers, 20 destroyers and numerous supply vessels. They were being followed by 10 big transports carrying some 30,000 to 40,000 Japanese troops, all headed toward the island of Midway.

On June 4, 1942, the three remaining United States carriers struck. In the furious Battle of Midway that followed, the Japanese Navy lost four of its five carriers, one cruiser, and three destroyers, suffering severe damage to two battleships, as well. The United States loss was the carrier *Yorktown* and one destroyer. The remains of the Japanese fleet hurriedly retreated back the way it had come.

Midway was the turning point of the war in the Pacific. Japan now lost its superiority in aircraft carriers, and thus its ability to cut supply lines to the United States land forces that were building up in Australia. In the months that followed, many more carriers came out of American shipyards, far outstripping the capacity of the Japanese to replace their losses.

Now Japan, in the Pacific, like Germany in Europe, found itself on the defensive in order to hold what it had won in the early days of the war.

Guadalcanal

The time had now come for American land forces to begin winning back the islands of the South Pacific that the Japanese had taken almost without opposition. The southernmost of these islands were the Solomons, chief among which was Guadalcanal, where the Japanese were completing an airfield.

After a violent barrage by naval guns and navy bombing planes, United States Marines landed on Guadalcanal in the first week of August, 1942. After a week of stiff fighting in the jungle, the Marines captured the airstrip and began to rebuild it for the use of American planes. But the Japanese troops, veterans of jungle fighting, retired into the hills and began a harassing defensive action.

In spite of the vigilance of United States ships offshore, thousands of

American soldier in the Guadalcanal jungle.

The American counterattack, which led to the reconquest of the Pacific, started with the landing of American troops on Guadalcanal and the landing of Australian and American troops on New Guinea.

Months of terrible, exhausting fighting in the jungle followed the landing on Guadalcanal.

Japanese troops were landed on the island to reinforce the garrison. The Marines—and later, Army troops—doggedly fought on, mopping up the island yard by yard. In the sea battles offshore—in which the Japanese attempted to land reinforcements and supplies, and the United States Navy was determined to prevent such a move—another Japanese carrier was sunk.

It was not until the middle of February that the Americans won a complete victory on Guadalcanal. But this was the first firm toehold on the long and bloody road to Tokyo.

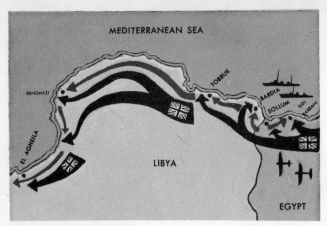

The British, by outflanking the Italians, trapped them at Sìdi Barrâni, Bardiyah, Tobruk, and Benghazi.

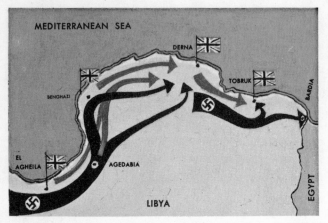

The territory lost by the Italians was regained by the Germans under Rommel.

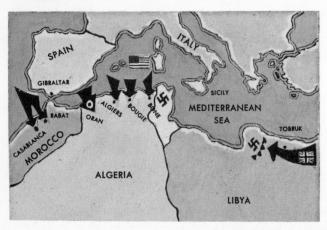

The beginning of defeat for the German armies started with the landing of Allied forces in North Africa.

The War in Africa

While Hitler's armies were running over Europe in the spring of 1940, Mussolini, in Italy, felt that he was being left out of things. His Axis partner was getting all the glory. He, too, wanted to be a conqueror. So he opened up the war on another front—North Africa.

His objective was Egypt, with its rich lands of the lower Nile delta, its great cities of Cairo and Alexandria and, most important, the Suez Canal. This vital waterway, which connected the Mediterranean with the Red Sea, was controlled by the British who prevented the Axis nations from using the canal. Its capture by the enemy would have been a tragic loss for the Allies.

In midsummer of 1940, Mussolini massed his armies in the Italian colony of Libya on the Egyptian frontier. From there, he struck out across the desert toward Alexandria.

Although Egypt was an independent country, the Egyptians had a treaty with Great Britain, whereby British troops were stationed there to protect the interests of both countries. The British were desperately short of men and fighting equipment, but they were hardened desert-fighters and determined to drive the Italians back.

The Italians, who were poorly trained, were thrown back clear across Libya in a disorderly retreat. The men surrendered in groups of thousands.

Hitler, gloating over his easy victory in France, and secretly planning at that time his attack on Russia, did not want to get involved in Africa. But there was nothing he could do except bail out his partner. Therefore, he sent German military units to go to Mussolini's aid. In command of this force was General Erwin Rommel, one of Hitler's ablest officers.

The British supply lines were extended so far from

The crew of a German tank surrenders to soldiers of the British Eighth Army during the North African campaign.

their bases in Egypt that they were unable to maintain enough food for the men, ammunition for the guns, and gasoline for the tanks. The British began to withdraw, though they left an Australian division in the town of Tobruk. These tough Australians, known later as the "Rats of Tobruk," stood their ground and were a constant danger to Rommel's army.

General Rommel, who was to become an expert in desert warfare, came to be known as the "Desert Fox," because he was able to flank British units without warning and destroy or capture them. It seemed impossible to stop his relentless surge toward Alexandria.

At last, when the British had withdrawn to a thin line of defense only a few miles from Alexandria, they sent another general to command their army. His name was Bernard Montgomery. Montgomery, a rugged and fearless fighter, was determined to stand his ground and then attack.

By clever planning, he managed to cut the enemy army up into several parts and then proceeded to annihilate them one by one. Now it was the Germans whose lines of supply were badly overextended. Rommel began a slow and stubborn retreat.

At about the same time that Montgomery began his counteroffensive, the first American Army to see action against the Germans landed on the northwest coast of Africa in Morocco and Algeria. It was under the command of General Dwight D. Eisenhower, who was later to become President of the United States. This army and Montgomery's British forces began converging on the Germans to trap them in a pincers movement.

It was a long, drawn-out, and bloody campaign. But on May 12, 1943, the last of the German Army surrendered to the British and Americans. North Africa was now in Allied hands.

The Italian Campaign

With the Germans now driven out of Africa, General Eisenhower, who had been named Supreme Commander of Allied Forces, proceeded to launch an amphibious attack upon the continent of Europe by way of Italy. The first landings were to take place on the island of Sicily, which looks on the map like a football about to be kicked by the Italian boot. The Allied armies were about to give it a much harder blow.

On July 10, 1943, the Allied invasion force of a quarter of a million men began their landings. For several weeks before, American and British bombers had been destroying coastal defenses, wiping out air bases, and blowing up harbors and railroad centers.

Italian soldiers, who had been driven into the war against their will by Mussolini, surrendered by the thousands. Many of them volunteered to help the Allied forces unload their supplies. The German troops, however, put up a stubborn defense, although they were outnumbered and outgunned. It was not until August 17 that the fighting ended.

General Eisenhower at once went on with his plans to take his huge army across the narrow Straits of Messina and invade the Italian mainland.

Even before Eisenhower completed his conquest of Sicily, the Italian Government had begun to cave in. Mussolini was ousted from his leadership and thrown into prison. A few weeks later, the new Italian regime surrendered to the Allies and declared war on Germany. The Germans rescued Mussolini from prison and set him up as leader in a puppet government in northern Italy, which

After defeating the Axis armies in North Africa, the victorious Allies turned their attention to the invasion of Europe. The first major assault was on the island of Sicily, bridge to the Italian mainland.

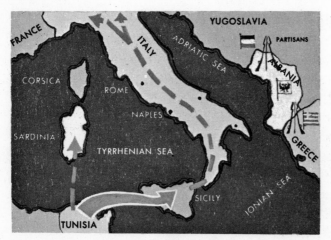

American soldiers, having established a beachhead on Sicily, evacuated their wounded and brought equipment ashore.

they occupied. In 1945, in an attempt to escape the advancing Allies, Mussolini was caught and shot by his own people. The Italian people had never wanted to go to war in the first place. Hitler had simply used Mussolini as a puppet.

Now, in September, 1943, the Allied armies hit the mainland of Italy. Slowly, relentlessly, they pushed their way northward. The German defenders fought them every agonizing step of the way.

When winter came, things had settled down to a sort of stalemate, with both opposing armies hammering at each other without mercy in the hills of southern Italy. But an even bigger explosion was being readied in northern Europe. So the Americans and the Germans were left to fight it out in Italy through a murderous winter and spring.

Advance in the Pacific

After their lightning strike against Pearl Harbor, the Japanese had moved swiftly down through the Pacific, snatching up British, American, and Dutch island possessions as they went. Although the small garrisons on these islands put up gallant defenses, the Japanese forces were overwhelming.

Before General Douglas MacArthur, the commanding officer in the Philippines, escaped from that island, he had made a dramatic and now-famous statement, "I shall return!" Now, he laid his plans to do so.

Australia and New Zealand, as parts of the British Commonwealth of Nations, had declared war on Italy, Germany, and Japan at the same time as Great Britain. Now Australia was to be used as the staging base for the re-conquest of the Pacific.

President Roosevelt had ordered General MacArthur to leave the Philippines by submarine in order to take supreme command.

Many observers did not see how it would be possible for the American forces to fight step by step up through the Pacific and drive out the Japanese, island by island and country by country. But MacArthur had no intention of trying to accomplish a bloody and laborious task.

His plan was to take only the strategic islands, on which airstrips for long-range bombers could be built, and bypass the others. The remaining Japanese forces in the Pacific would be left to "die on the vine." With their supplies cut off by the American advance, the Japanese would be forced into surrender or starvation.

The advance began after the first success in the Solomons. From there, American amphibious forces, by now vastly superior to the Japanese, began a deadly game of island-hopping up the Pacific islands. It was a long and bloody battle, and the Americans suffered heavy casualties in exchange for every island they took.

After the Solomons came the reconquest, by the Army, Navy, and Marine Corps, of New Guinea, the Gilbert Islands, the Marshalls, Palau, the Marianas, the Philippines, Iwo Jima, and finally — Okinawa.

Okinawa was on the front doorstep of Japan's main island group, and here the Japanese made their last and hardest-fought stand. It was in this battle that the Japanese Air Force first introduced its *kamakazi*, or suicide, planes as a last desperate resort.

Pressed into the defensive, the Japanese became more and more desperate. Kamikaze planes, filled with explosives, were crash-dived onto the decks of American carriers by Japanese pilots.

181

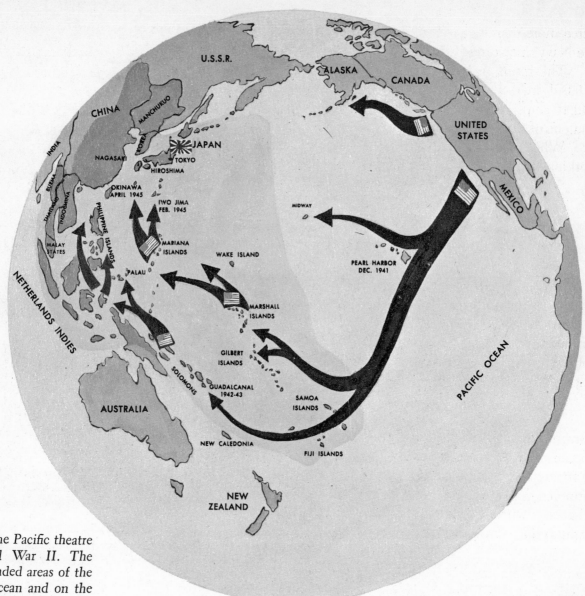

Map of the Pacific theatre in World War II. The darker shaded areas of the Pacific Ocean and on the continent of Asia mark the extent of the farthest Japanese expansion.

The *kamakazi* planes were unarmored, and their pilots had no training beyond getting the planes off the ground and controlling them in the air. Each *kamakazi* carried one bomb, and the mission of the pilot was to dive his plane into an American ship, deliberately sacrificing his own life in the process. A few made hits, but most were knocked down by American planes or anti-aircraft fire.

The battle for Okinawa, the final one of the Pacific war, began on April 1, 1945, and lasted for 83 days. The American invading forces numbered more than a quarter of a million men, backed up by 1,300 ships of the Navy, including battleships and aircraft carriers.

The result was an extremely high casualty rate for the Japanese: 110,071 men were killed, 7,400 captured, and they lost 7,830 aircraft and 16 ships, one of which was the *Yamato*, the world's largest battleship and one of the very few fighting ships remaining in the Japanese Navy.

When the frightful Battle of Okinawa finally came to an end, nothing stood in the way of a final American assault on Japan itself.

Invasion of France and Germany

In the months that followed the attack on Pearl Harbor and America's entrance into the war against the Axis, the United States began building up its military power in England. By the middle of 1942, long-range bombers of the United States, along with planes of Great Britain's Royal Air Force, were making daily raids over Germany.

The Americans bombed by day and the British by night. This arrangement was made because the American planes, like the *Flying Fortress* and the *Liberator*, were more strongly armored than the British bombers and had a better chance of withstanding the attacks of the German fighters that came up in the daytime to meet them.

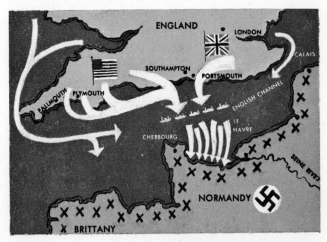

Under the protection of air and naval forces, the Allied armies crossed the English Channel for the invasion of Normandy on the northwest coast of France. This was D-Day, June 6, 1944.

By 1944, Allied bombers were smashing hard at German industrial centers. Hamburg, center of Nazi submarine production, was almost totally destroyed. As the bombing increased in fury, other cities such as Dresden, Essen, and Dusseldorf were leveled.

Then, the United States developed fighter-escort planes that could fly almost as far as the big bombers, and the range of the bombing raids was lengthened. Now the Germans were getting back a severe dose of their own medicine. Some of the missions were extremely long and all of them were dangerous. German anti-aircraft fire harassed the bombers all the way through German-held territory. Swarms of *Luftwaffe* fighters flew from German airfields to shoot them down.

But although the losses in British and American aircraft were appallingly high, Germany's industries were slowly being wiped out. With one raid on Regensburg, where most of the ball-bearings for Nazi airplanes were manufactured, American bombers virtually brought Geman airplane production to a standstill.

American ground forces, as well as air forces, were also building up in England. It was obvious that a direct land invasion of France would be necessary before the war could be finally won. Furthermore, the Russians were demanding a "second front" to take some of the pressure off their own hard-pressed armies. General Eisenhower was brought from the Italian theater of war as Supreme Commander of the combined Allied armies.

For many months, vast stockpiles of supplies — big guns, tanks, mortars, trucks, mountains of ammunition, fuel, and food — had been accumulated for the attack. Hundreds of thousands of soldiers were especially trained in landing techniques. Thousands of landing craft were assembled to be ready at a moment's notice. The invasion was given the code name of "Operation Overlord." The date for the big push was set for June 6, 1944. This was known as D-Day. (The "D" stands for the first letter of the word "day.")

The invasion of the Normandy coast, after repeated attacks from the air had softened the enemy's defense, began with the landing of Allied troops from special assault ships.

In the early morning of D-Day, thousands of British and American bombers dropped tens of thousands of tons of bombs on German defense positions along the French coast of Normandy. Then, the infantry came in, wave after wave, in assault boats, and hit the beaches at five different points. They dug in under heavy German fire and then proceeded to push inland.

All that day, and the next and the next and the next, the invasion forces poured into Normandy. Slowly, painfully, fighting furiously for every foot of ground, the American, British, and Canadians advanced their columns into France. The German defenders did not give an inch without a fight. But they were outmanned and outgunned, and were outnumbered ten to one in the air. Even so, the *Wehrmacht* put up their stiffest fight of the war.

The invading Allied armies fanned out in half a dozen directions at once. Thousands of men and thousands of tons of heavy equipment were landed on the Normandy beachheads every day, and the armies of the Allies grew stronger as they surged ahead.

Throughout much of Europe, scenes of ruin and devastation caused by the war were common sights.

House by house, farm by farm, the British and American soldiers fought their way through villages with such names as Caen, Bayeux, Carentan, St. Lô, Falaise, and St. Sauveur-de-Comte — names that have gone down in history. As they passed, the land behind them lay in ruins. But at long last, it was free.

The invading army swept east, and after two months of bitter fighting, its advance units entered Paris. An armored division, made up of Frenchmen who had managed to escape from the German occupation, was given the honor of being the first to enter the city. The Parisians lined the sidewalks and cheered them wildly, waving the French flags that they had kept carefully hidden ever since the Germans had come. The German garrison in Paris surrendered on August 25, 1944.

Six columns of British, Canadian, and American troops now stormed across all of France, sweeping back the Germans as they went. Two other armies drove up out of Italy, pushing the *Wehrmacht* ahead of them. Hitler's armies were in full retreat. But it was an orderly retreat, and they fought desperately for every bit of ground they gave.

But the *Wehrmacht* had not lost its will to fight back. In December, Field Marshal von Rundstedt, the German commander, amassed the best of his remaining forces and prepared them for one final, last-ditch effort to force the Allies back. He attacked the weakest part of the Americans' advancing line in the Forest of Ardennes, which lies in Belgium and Luxembourg. His plan was to split his attackers in two.

Von Rundstedt's counterattack hit the American Army on the foggy morning of December 16, 1944. Snow lay thick on the ground beneath the trees. Taken completely by surprise, a large segment of the American Army was quickly surrounded and cut off from its supply bases.

After the fighting on the Rhine River ended in an Allied victory, Allied armies poured into Germany. Russian troops entered the besieged Nazi homeland from the east.

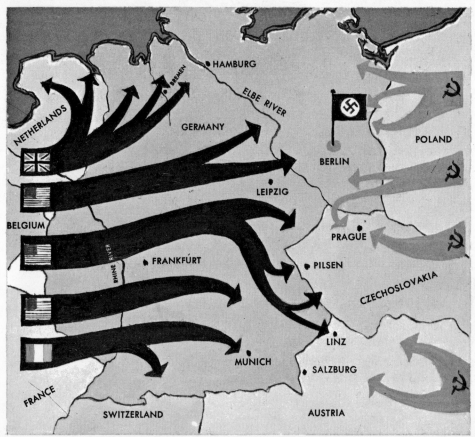

186

To make matters worse, some German soldiers were dressed in American uniforms and were able to speak English with an American accent. Penetrating the American lines, they issued fake orders to isolated units, which compounded the confusion.

For nearly three weeks, it looked like the old, successful *blitzkrieg* tactics, with German tank columns thundering over the snowy landscape and gobbling up small American units. Then, Allied reinforcements were rushed in, and the German *blitz* was turned back.

After the Battle of the Bulge — as the Nazi counterattack in the Ardennes was called — the Germans began their long, slow retreat back into Germany. They crossed the Rhine and then prepared to defend it.

German engineers destroyed most of the Rhine bridges behind them. But in their haste, they waited too long to blow up the great Ludendorff Bridge at Remagen. American advance elements took advantage of this mistake, and quickly threw several divisions across the river. Now Allied invaders were on German soil for the first time.

German bombers managed to blow up the bridge at Remagen a few days later. But by this time, the Americans had built pontoon bridges, and the advance into Germany continued at a quickening pace.

On the "holy soil," as the Germans called their own country, they fought even harder than they had in France. But it was impossible for them to hold back the flood of the Allied attack.

All through the winter and spring of 1944-45, the last German strongholds fell one by one. Finally, there was only Berlin.

The Fall of Berlin

While British and American Armies were driving the Germans out of France and back into their own country, the Russians were doing the same thing from the east. The German assault on Russia, which Hitler had said would be a quick and easy victory, had turned into a nightmare.

German armor bogged down in the deep Russian snows. Supply lines were cut. The *Wehrmacht* did not have enough food for its men nor ammunition for its guns. On the other hand, the Russians had been receiving lend-lease supplies from the United States, and as the Germans grew weaker, the Russians grew stronger. The Germans who managed to survive straggled back along the bleak road to Berlin.

Now, what was left of the once-fearsome German Army was caught between two irresistible forces, the British and Americans on one side and the Russians on the other. Men abandoned their equipment and began to surrender by the hundreds of thousands.

As the ruthless ring of fire and steel closed in on Berlin itself, Adolph Hitler, who had once proudly boasted that he would dictate to all Europe — and the world — shot himself in an underground bomb shelter. All around him the once great German capital lay in ruins, the shattered victim of Allied bombs.

On V-E Day (Victory-in-Europe Day), May 7, 1945, the last of the German Armies surrendered and the war in Europe was ended.

Victory in Japan

Ever since the American occupation of the Marianas, Iwo Jima, and Okinawa, the main Japanese islands had been under constant bombardment by long-range bombers of the United States. The city of Tokyo was leveled by day-and-night fire-bomb raids, as were many other important Japanese cities. As Italy and Germany had already done, Japan was paying the price for its grandiose plans for world conquest.

Then the United States unveiled the biggest surprise in all the history of warfare. It was the deadliest weapon ever designed — the atomic bomb.

Work on this dreadful bomb, which cost about two billion dollars to produce, had begun in 1940. The work had been done in the utmost secrecy, and very few people knew about it.

It was known that Germany was experimenting with such a bomb, so American scientists worked furiously to win the atomic race. The United States succeeded in winning because the nation had better scientific equipment, more money to spend and, most important, gifted scientists. In fact, many scientists who had been forced to flee from Germany and Nazi-occupied Europe worked on the atomic energy program for the United States.

Even after the bomb had been perfected, there was a great deal of controversy among our scientific, military, and political leaders about whether it should be used. It was sure to kill thousands of civilians and unleash a horrible force for destruction upon the world.

But most of the people in Washington argued that the use of the atomic bomb would bring a quick end to the war and save as many as a hundred thousand American lives in the event that a direct invasion had to be made on Japan.

On August 6, 1945, the world's first atomic bomb was dropped on the Japanese city of Hiroshima by an American B-29 bomber. This one blast, with an explosive force of 20,000 tons of TNT, and released by the touch of one man's finger on a control, left the city in almost total ruins. Three days later, a second atomic bomb was dropped on the city of Nagasaki.

With such weapons in American hands, the Japanese gave up all hope of winning the war. They surrendered on V-J Day (Victory-over-Japan Day), September 2, 1945.

Now the long, bloody war was over, and the whole world breathed a sigh of thanksgiving. Hitler and Mussolini were dead. The Emperor of Japan declared publicly that he was not a god, but a human being without divine power.

But the war had cost a terrible price. The dead numbered in the millions, and the homeless, in the hundreds of millions. Vast areas of Europe and Asia were left in ruins. In terms of money alone, that price had been almost one-and-a-half *trillion* dollars. Yet, at last, the world was at peace again.

The most devastating weapon of all, the atomic bomb, was developed by America. It hastened the end of the war with Japan and saved many American lives by avoiding the necessity of an invasion into Japan.

The War-Crimes Trials

After the war had ended, a number of Axis leaders were accused and brought to trial for "crimes against humanity." These crimes were mainly brutal acts against innocent civilians that went far beyond the normal waging of a war against soldiers and military targets.

These crimes, most of which were committed by the Nazis, included the deliberate killing of civilians and prisoners of war; the sinking of un-armed ships; the torpedoing of hospital ships that were clearly marked with the Red Cross; the roundup of helpless civilians and military pris-oners for slave labor; the needless destruction of entire cities, towns, and villages; and the ruthless plunder and looting of public and private property.

The most horrible of these crimes was the wholesale slaughter of Jewish people in Germany and in the German-occupied countries. Men, women, and children were rounded up and taken out to the forests to be shot, or they were taken to such Nazi concentration camps as Auschwitz, Dachau, and Buchenwald, and there brutally murdered in gas chambers. During this period of unspeakable horror, 6,000,000 Jews were put to death by the German Nazis. The dead included 1,000,000 children.

The Jews were not the only people to suffer. In every country that the Nazis occupied, other innocent people — and freedom — perished. Hitler was also opposed to Christianity and planned to create in its place a Nazi religion in which the sword and the swastika, and not the Christian cross, would be the new symbols.

The Allies decided that the people who were responsible for the atrocities and for deliberately starting and waging warfare should be tried, and if convicted, punished. Many war crimes trials were held, the most important of which took place at Nuremberg, Germany. Another was held at Tokyo, Japan. Most of the defendants were found guilty and hanged.

The United Nations

With total victory by the Allies now finally won, the war-weary world turned to the task of picking up its pieces and putting itself back together.

In the late fall of 1944 and the early spring of 1945 — before the war was actually over, but when the end was clearly in sight — representatives of the United States, Russia, Great Britain, and China set the groundwork for an organization that was to be called the United Nations. This name had first been suggested by the United States President, Franklin D. Roosevelt.

The object of this international body was to make sure that another World War would never happen again. All disputes between countries were to be settled in the United Nations by peaceful means. The invention of the atomic bomb, which could wipe out whole nations at a single blow, made another war unthinkable.

Today, the United Nations has its headquarters in New York City. Almost all the nations of the world — from every continent — are member states.

Although international tension exists once more in the world — between the Communists on one side and the free nations on the other — the United Nations has been a means thus far of averting total war.

All the peace-loving people of the world pray that the United Nations will continue to play this vital role — and that no historian of the future will ever have to write a book about "World War III."

Highlights: 1922-1945

1922
Oct. 30   Fascist "March on Rome," a revolutionary uprising of Mussolini's Fascist party.
Oct. 31   Mussolini becomes prime minister of Italy — and dictator.

1931
Sept. 18   Japanese invade Manchuria.

1933
Jan. 30   Hitler becomes chancellor of Germany — and dictator.

1935
March 16   Hitler re-establishes universal military training in Germany.
Oct. 3   Italy invades Ethiopia.

1936
March 7   Hitler remilitarizes the Rhineland, defying Versailles Treaty.
July 17   Spanish Civil war begins.
Oct. 1   Franco becomes Spain's head.
Oct. 27   Hitler and Mussolini form the Rome-Berlin Axis.
Nov. 18   The Axis powers recognize Franco's dictatorial regime in Spain.
Nov. 25   Japan and Germany sign anti-Comintern treaty.

1937
July 7   Japan invades China.
Nov. 6   Italy adheres to German-Japanese anti-Comintern treaty.

1938
March 11   Germans enter Austria.
March 12   Austria declared part of German Reich (Anschluss).

Oct. 29   Munich conference.

1939
April 7   Italy invades Albania.
April 28   Hitler denounces German-Polish non-aggression pact.
Aug. 23   Non-aggression pact signed between Russia and Germany.
Aug. 29   Germany demands city of Danzig from Poland.
Sept. 1   Germany invades Poland.
Sept. 3   Britain, Australia, New Zealand and France declare war on Germany.
Sept. 17   Russia invades east Poland.
Sept. 28   Germany and Russia arrange to divide Poland between them.
Nov. 24   Japanese sever China from French Indochina.
Nov. 30   Russia invades Finland.

1940
April 9   Germany invades Denmark and Norway.
May 10   Germany invades Belgium, Luxembourg and Holland.
May 12   Germany invades France.
May 26-June 3   Dunkirk evacuated.
June 10   Italy declares war on France and Great Britain.
June 22   France surrenders.
Aug. 4   Italy invades Br. Somaliland.
Sept. 22   Japanese begin invasion of French Indochina.
Sept. 27   Three-Power Pact between Germany, Italy and Japan.
Oct. 28   Italy invades Greece.
Nov. 20   Hungary joins the Axis.
Nov. 23   Romania joins the Axis.

1941
April 6   Germany invades Yugoslavia and Greece.
April 13   Japan and Soviet Union sign a non-aggression treaty.
April 17   Yugoslavia surrenders to Axis. Tito organizes guerrillas.
June 22   Germany invades Russia.
July 13   Great Britain and Russia sign mutual-aid treaty.
Aug. 14   The Atlantic Charter.
Aug. 25   British and Russian troops occupy Iran.
Dec. 7   Japan attacks Pearl Harbor.
Dec. 8   The United States Congress declares war on Japan.
Dec. 10   Guam surrenders to Japan.
Dec. 11   Germany and Italy declare war on the United States. The United States Congress declares war on Germany and Italy.
Dec. 23   Wake Island surrenders to Japan.
Dec. 25   British in Hong Kong surrender to Japanese, who continue to extend pressure on Southeast Asia.

1942
Jan. 2   Manila falls to Japan.
Jan. 11   Japanese forces land in the Dutch East Indies.
Feb. 8   Burma invaded by Japanese.
Feb. 15   Singapore, in Malaya, surrenders to Japan.
Feb. 27   The Allies lose the Battle of the Java Sea.
March 7   Dutch East Indies occupied by Japan.
April 9   Bataan falls to Japan.

April 18 U. S. aircraft raid Tokyo.
May 4-8 The Allies win the Battle of the Coral Sea.
May 6 Corregidor falls to Japan.
June 3-6 The Allies win the Battle of Midway.
June 21 Germans seize Tobruk.
July 2 The British stop the German advance at El Alamein.
Aug. 7 American marines land on the island of Guadalcanal.
Oct. 23-Nov. 3 Britain takes the offensive at El Alamein.
Nov. 7-8 Allies land in North Africa.
Nov. 12 British retake Tobruk.
Nov. 19 Beginning of Russian counter-offensive near Stalingrad.

1943

Jan. 14-24 Casablanca conference.
Feb. 2 German defeat at Stalingrad.
March 13 Japanese forces in China retreat across the Yangtze River.
May 12 Axis defeated in Africa.
May 23 Japanese end their resistance on Attu in the Aleutian Islands.
July 10 Allies invade island of Sicily.
July 26 Mussolini resigns and is placed under arrest. Marshal Badoglio dissolves Fascist party and forms new Italian government.
Sept. 3 The Allies land on Italian mainland. Italian government signs armistice agreement with the Allies.
Sept. 13 General Chiang Kai-shek elected president of China.
Oct. 13 Italy declares war on Nazi Germany.
Nov. 1 American troops land on Bougainville in the Solomon Islands.
Nov. 20 United States marines land on Makin and Tarawa.

Nov. 22-26 Roosevelt, Churchill and Chiang Kai-shek confer at Cairo, Egypt. They pledge defeat of Japan and liberation of Korea.
Nov. 28-Dec. 1 Roosevelt, Churchill and Stalin agree on invasion of Europe at Teheran conference in Iran.

1944

Jan. 27 Russian army stops German attack on Leningrad.
Jan. 31 United States forces attack Kwajalein atoll.
Feb. 17 United States Navy raids Truk Island.
Feb. 29 Allied forces land in the Admiralty Islands.
March 19 Germany invades Hungary.
March 22 Japan invades India.
June 6 D-day in Europe.
June 15-July 9 The United States wins the Battle of Saipan.
June 15-16 B-29's begin strategic bombing of Japanese mainland.
June 19-20 United States Navy wins the Battle of the Philippine Sea.
July 20-Aug. 3 Guam reconquered by United States forces.
Aug. 25 Paris is liberated.
Sept. 15-Oct. 13 United States forces invade Palau Islands.
Oct. 20 U. S. Army lands on Leyte.
Oct. 23-26 Decisive defeat of the Japanese navy by the United States Pacific Fleet in the Battle for Leyte Gulf in Philippine Sea.
Dec. 16 The Germans start counter-offensive (Battle of the Bulge).
Dec. 27 The Allies stop German offensive at Battle of the Bulge.

1945

Jan. 9 United States troops land on Luzon in the Philippines.
Jan. 21 Hungary declares war on Nazi Germany.
Jan. 22 A land route to China is opened by Allies.
Feb. 11 Roosevelt, Churchill and Stalin sign Yalta agreement, dealing with post-war problems.
Feb. 13 Russians occupy Budapest, capital of Hungary.
Feb. 19 United States Marines land on Iwo Jima.
April 1 United States forces land on Okinawa.
April 12 President Roosevelt dies; Truman becomes President.
April 13 Russians invade Vienna.
April 25 Troops of United States and Russia meet at Torgau, Germany.
April 28 Mussolini is executed.
May 1 German forces in Italy surrender to Allies.
May 1 Suicide of Hitler announced.
May 2 Berlin falls to Russian units.
May 7 V-E day: Germany surrenders at Reims, France.
July 17-Aug. 2 The Allies issue the Potsdam Declaration (preparation of peace plans).
Aug. 6 Atomic bomb dropped on Hiroshima, Japan.
Aug. 9 Atomic bomb dropped on Nagasaki, Japan.
Sept. 2 V-J-day: Japan signs surrender terms aboard **Missouri.**
Sept. 8 Japanese military units in China surrender.
Sept. 12 Japanese forces in Southeast Asia surrender.
Oct. 24 United Nations established.